Palgrave Texts in Counselling and Psychotherapy

Series Editors

David Pocock
Psychoanalytic Psychotherapist & Systematic Family Therapist
Calne, Wiltshire, UK

Jeremy Woodcock
Holman's Cottage
Nailsworth, UK

This series introduces readers to the theory and practice of counselling and psychotherapy across a wide range of topical issues. Ideal for both trainees and practitioners, the books will appeal to anyone wishing to use counselling and psychotherapeutic skills and will be particularly relevant to workers in health, education, social work and related settings. The books in this series emphasise an integrative orientation weaving together a variety of models including, psychodynamic, attachment, trauma, narrative and systemic ideas. The books are written in an accessible and readable style with a focus on practice. Each text offers theoretical background and guidance for practice, with creative use of clinical examples.

Caryn Onions • Heather Price
Dave Roberts

Supporting Children and Young People with Complex Needs

palgrave
macmillan

Caryn Onions
The Mulberry Bush Organisation
Standlake, Oxfordshire, UK

Heather Price
The Open University
Milton Keynes, UK

Dave Roberts
The Mulberry Bush Organisation
Standlake, Oxfordshire, UK

ISSN 2662-9127 ISSN 2662-9135 (electronic)
Palgrave Texts in Counselling and Psychotherapy
ISBN 978-3-032-16698-2 ISBN 978-3-032-16699-9 (eBook)
https://doi.org/10.1007/978-3-032-16699-9

Cover credit: Zoonar GmbH

This Palgrave Macmillan imprint is published by the registered company Springer Nature Switzerland AG.
The registered company address is: Gewerbestrasse 11, 6330 Cham, Switzerland

Foreword

The first children to live at the Mulberry Bush in 1948 would now be 90 years old, and some of them are potentially great-grandparents. When I first became involved in therapeutic care for children who have suffered trauma and other adversities, we talked about breaking the cycle of deprivation and abuse, so that young people who had suffered might flourish and raise their children healthily. In this sense, the value of breaking the cycle goes on from one generation to the next. The founder of the Mulberry Bush, Barbara Dockar-Drysdale, and her husband Stephen, and those who have followed, have much to be commended for.

The work of the Mulberry Bush has spread far, shining a light on the possibility of growth and recovery from the most adverse childhood circumstances. While large numbers of children have benefited, the same is true for many of those who worked with them. I had the good fortune of working with Dockar-Drysdale when she became the consultant child psychotherapist at the Cotswold Community, a residential therapeutic community for boys.

I remember when she was asked in a team consultation if she believed in life after death. She answered that we live on through the people who have internalised something of their connection with us.

Writing about this work provides another opportunity for people close and afar to learn something of value, through reflection and by relating the ideas to their own experience. That which is written and recorded can be revisited or found for the first time decades later. Dockar-Drysdale and others who followed at the Mulberry Bush, such as Richard Rollinson, Christopher Reeves, and John Diamond, have carried on this tradition.

And of course, as referred to in this book, the work of Donald Winnicott had a huge influence on Dockar-Drysdale, the Mulberry Bush, the Cotswold Community, as well as many other therapeutic residential care organisations. More widely across the world, Winnicott may be best known for the term he introduced in 1953, the 'good-enough mother' or parent, which has influenced the way we think about the role of parents.

The task in the here and now of enabling children to recover from serious adversity, to grow, and to flourish is always our main concern. However, we can never underestimate the knock-on benefits for everyone who is involved, what they learn, and how they develop. And how their journeys will touch upon the lives of so many others who may never have set foot in the Mulberry Bush School. In this way, the continuing existence of the Mulberry Bush for nearly eighty years offers a beacon of hope.

This book is completed as the Mulberry Bush nears its 80th anniversary. It carries on a tradition but also adds something creative and new. There must be a reason why the Mulberry Bush has lasted so long when so many other allied organisations are sadly no longer with us. As well as having generations of dedicated and effective leaders and staff, from the start, the Mulberry Bush has had a clear model of how to work with children. Like any successful organisation, it has also adapted effectively throughout the decades, with many ups and downs, and serious challenges. A core aim for the Mulberry Bush is for everyone to learn from experience. Ainsworth and Hansen (2008, p. 44) proposed that residential services need to be 'dynamic living and learning environments'. I hope that this book, alongside the history of the Mulberry Bush, is an example of such a 'place'.

The book covers the key elements involved in therapeutic work. The chapters are chosen to provide a coherent whole. The authors combine many excellent case illustrations to bring alive the nature of the work with children, young people, and their families. They also make it clear that we must pay significant attention to the support and development of the staff, whatever their role. Emphasis is placed on the value of making sense of what may seem and feel unthinkable. The overall approach is fundamentally relational. The authors combine attachment, psychodynamic, and neuroscience theories to help understand the needs of the children and the impact of the work.

The book moves between the details of work with children and macro issues of the organisational context and research. The authors make it clear that there must be reflective processes, and these must be modelled at all levels of the organisation. In the introduction of the book, Price and Onions ask,

> What is the state of mind needed to hold the 'mess' when things go awry'? By 'state of mind' we are focussing on the state of mind of the organisation and/or team and/or member of staff.

In many ways, the book is an answer to this question at all levels: from the individual worker to the organisation. We need to be as well prepared as possible to provide and maintain a receptive state of mind. If we are not well prepared, traumatised young people will most likely, through unconscious communicative processes, help to recreate the states of mind in us that they are familiar with. Emotional reactivity, detachment, and sometimes harsh punishment by their previous caregivers are common. This book encourages us to aim for a state of mind where we can pay thoughtful attention in order to maintain a presence that is kind and curious, can remain grounded amongst turmoil, that can adjust and adapt. These are the aims that the Mulberry Bush has embedded in its culture for nearly 80 years.

Patrick Tomlinson

Reference

Ainsworth, F., & Hansen, P. (2008). Programs for high needs children and young people: Group homes are not enough. *Children Australia*, *3*(2), 41–47.

Patrick Tomlinson is Director and Consultant specialising in Leadership and Organisational Development, and Children's Trauma Services Specialist. Beginning as a residential care worker, his roles have included senior leadership positions, consultant, and mentor. He is the author of numerous publications.

Acknowledgements

We would like to thank all the children, young people and organisations that we have worked with. It is through them that we have gained the experience needed to write about the work of the Mulberry Bush.

Our sincere thanks go to Dawn Davidson, Siobhan Foster-Weston and Mike Staines for their chapters. We are grateful for their support, commitment and good humour throughout the writing endeavour. We are also grateful to Patrick Tomlinson for his wise foreword, encouragement and international contributions to services for traumatised children.

Our sincere thanks also to the many colleagues and kind people who have given their time and energy to read parts of the manuscript. We are grateful to Geraldine Ackerman, Rita Baptista, Hannah Chapman, Anne-Marie Cummins, Clare Dorer, Polly Francis, Jo Kelsall, Kristie Langhoff, Jon Reid and Jen Roberts. Their comments, suggestions and support were invaluable in helping us shape this book. We thank Laura Pemberton for permission to quote from her action research and April Gold and Jessica Moore for their involvement and permission to use the Beacon Project as a case study in Chap. 10. Heartfelt thanks go to colleagues Ruth Kibble and John Turberville, who read the completed manuscript and offered detailed comments and thoughtful reflections.

Particular appreciation goes to past pupils and families from the Mulberry Bush, especially Shirlee Davies, Sally Finch and Taygen Kelleher for their invaluable contributions.

We also appreciate the continuing support and commitment of our colleagues across the Mulberry Bush and those too numerous to mention who no longer work at the Mulberry Bush, but whose contribution lives on. Finally, we would like to thank Angie Brown for her support in getting this project over the finish line.

Competing Interests The authors have no competing interests to declare that are relevant to the content of this manuscript.

Praise for *Supporting Children and Young People with Complex Needs*

"This book is a vital resource for anyone working with vulnerable children and young people. It moves beyond simplistic solutions to offer a deeply insightful, relational approach rooted in understanding the complex interplay of trauma, attachment and communication. Through compelling case studies and practical frameworks, the authors provide a roadmap for building therapeutic relationships and fostering a more compassionate and effective system of care. A must-read for educators, social workers, therapists, and anyone committed to creating a more supportive world for children who struggle."

—Fatima Whitbread MBE, *Founder of Fatima's UK Campaign, London, UK*

"This book is a carefully crafted, practical and evidence-informed guide to working with children and young people on the edge of school and family life. Drawing upon the long and rich history of the Mulberry Bush's uniquely successful model of supporting children in the context of a residential school and children's home, this book offers clear insights into children's complex needs and behaviours. With empathy and care both for children and the professionals who support them across a range of disciplines and settings, the authors provide practical advice for how to better meet the needs of children in ways that keep staff (and the environments in which they work with children) safe and supported. Written carefully, compassionately and compellingly, this book will be immensely useful for anyone working with and caring for children – in all of the complexity and vivacity of their present selves – and the hope and potential for their futures."

—Kristine Langhoff, *Professor of Social Work (Social Work and Social Care), UK*

"This is a very accessible and important text that helps readers engage with and more deeply understand the task of supporting children to heal from trauma. Drawing on a wide range of case vignettes, from different contexts, we are helped to consider what is going on beneath the surface of what we see, and then to consider not only how different staff might respond in theoretically informed ways, but also what other factors need to be considered and managed in the system around children and practitioners. A valuable contribution to support this much needed focus on evidenced based, relational work – beneficial for commissioners and providers alike."

—Kevin Gallagher, *Managing Director Amberleigh Care, UK*

Contents

List of Figures

CHAPTER 1

Introduction

Heather Price and Caryn Onions

This is a book about working with children and young people who are on the edge of school and family life. Here, we are thinking about children in and on the edge of the care system, and children with complex social, emotional, mental health and disability needs, whose anxiety and/or behaviour places them at particular risk of exclusion. It is about the struggle to help these children as well as help those who face the profound challenges of looking after them.

Since 2020 the UK has seen a 140% increase in children needing special educational needs support. The areas with particularly high levels of need are social, emotional and mental health; disabilities; and speech, language and communication (National Audit Office, 2024). Children in and on the edge of the care system ('children in need' and 'children looked after') are particularly vulnerable: they are twice as likely to have special educational needs and are much more likely to be excluded from school (Department for Education, 2025). Child and Adolescent Mental Health Services are under increasing pressure (Stafford et al., 2020), with long waiting lists for appointments (Children's Commissioner, 2024), and social services are experiencing increasing referrals of children with complex needs and behavioural difficulties at a time when real resources are decreasing (Institute for Government, 2023).

This book outlines a therapeutic, relational approach to working with children. It re-thinks what 'therapy' can be—not an hour-long session of

C. Onions et al., *Supporting Children and Young People with Complex Needs*, Palgrave Texts in Counselling and Psychotherapy, https://doi.org/10.1007/978-3-032-16699-9_1

treatment, or even necessarily talking about feelings, but finding a way of working that builds a relationship with the individual child and allows that child, slowly and incrementally, to speak about their issues when the timing feels right for them. Central to this way of working is building a parallel team around the person who is holding the child in mind, so they are well supported.

This approach has been developed at the Mulberry Bush charity in its residential school and children's home based in Oxfordshire, UK. The charity provides specialist therapeutic support and outreach services to those troubled and traumatised as children, and the authors of this book met through their work and involvement with the Mulberry Bush. Since 2011, the Mulberry Bush's approach has been taken out to a variety of settings through the outreach team and consulting service, which provides training in mainstream and special schools, children's homes and the secure estate, in the UK and internationally. The Mulberry Bush was founded in 1948 and has sustained a therapeutic community approach throughout that time.

We have written for a range of professionals who share a common interest, concern, passion, enthusiasm and energy to support these young people. They may be people who work in schools, social and health care, residential and secure settings, foster care or adoption, and anyone else curious about therapeutic work based on relational practice. This book is for practitioners who work closely with children and who need to rely on their relationship with the child to enable the work to happen, irrespective of the work setting.

We use case studies and practice examples to illustrate a variety of situations where children and young people struggle to feel they belong, and where their behaviour is perplexing and upsetting. We also include the voice of past Mulberry Bush pupils as experts by experience.

The authors have personal and professional experience of supporting children and young people in the care system, in education, in foster, adoption and residential care, as well as child mental health and youth justice. Using the core principles of the therapeutic approach at the Mulberry Bush—namely, psychodynamic and systemic theory, collaborative working and reflective practice—the authors have used examples of recurring challenges experienced by children, families and colleagues to highlight opportunities for these difficult and painful situations to be thought about, addressed and discussed.

This book is not meant to be a manual telling you 'how to do the work' or suggesting specific interventions for different age groups or situations. Instead, we share with you the dilemmas we have encountered and the ways in which we have deliberated and thought about the difficulties of the children and young people. It is not, therefore, a handbook that will give you answers but instead will share with you some common practice dilemmas that we have experienced in different settings and how we have approached them.

You may be wondering why we did not write a handbook. Perhaps that would have been more straightforward. However, our decision to write the book in this way comes from our experience of working with staff in many different settings outside of the Mulberry Bush, both in the UK and abroad.

Over the years, we have been contacted by numerous organisations struggling to help staff and children while at the same time wanting to implement a therapeutic approach. We often find that these enquiries boil down to a few similar broad themes. Usually, high up on the list, people ask how we manage children's 'bad' behaviour and how we get them to do what staff say. There is then a second theme about staff training and support and how the organisation is arranged to get the most from the workforce. We repeatedly find ourselves giving a similar answer, which can be summarised as 'what is the state of mind needed to hold the 'mess' when things go awry'? By 'state of mind' we are focusing on the state of mind of the organisation and/or team and/or member of staff. I expect our reply might sometimes be disappointing or puzzling, as it is not about what sanctions or rules to put in place. Instead, we emphasise that helping children and young people who have experienced complex trauma can be messy and complicated, especially if staff teams have not been authorised or do not have the skills to delve into it.

We by no means want to suggest that we have all the answers or that it is easy work. In fact, it is because we recognise how complicated the work can be when all the people involved might be feeling confused, overwhelmed, hurt, ashamed and inadequate that we decided to focus on how we think about and respond to these challenges rather than suggest specific interventions or programmes of work. What we want is for practitioners to think about the difficulties in their setting, see how they might approach the situation, and consider how they can adopt a different or new 'state of mind' rather than introduce a new intervention.

At the Mulberry Bush, we have developed our model of practice through working in teams. We acknowledge that we are in a different position to some other supportive people such as foster carers and adopters, who might have little if any daily support from people close to hand. We hope that they might see a way in which they could adapt our approach to their understanding of the child and their network.

We are using composite practice examples in this book to maintain confidentiality for the children, young people, families and organisations we have worked with. A composite example is a practice-based case study that combines elements from multiple people's experiences to form a single, illustrative story. The different components of the narrative may all be true, but they have been brought together to create a made-up example. Where we have permission from individuals to use actual material this is acknowledged.

Outline of the Book

In Chap. 2, Roots of the Mulberry Bush Approach, Heather Price and Caryn Onions discuss the wider relevance of the three practice-based principles underpinning the work of the Mulberry Bush. The first principle, a psychodynamic approach, is explained as looking 'under the surface' of behaviour to better understand it. The second principle introduced is a systemic, collaborative approach which assumes the 'whole' is greater than the sum of its parts when professionals work together. The third principle, reflective practice, is described as needing to take seriously support for processing the emotional load of working alongside children with complex needs. The latter half of the chapter revisits two enduring concepts from the work of the founder of the Mulberry Bush, Barbara Dockar-Drysdale. These are 'the provision of primary experience' and 'the management of violence'.

In Chap. 3, New Beginnings, Dawn Davidson and Siobhan Foster-Weston consider new children and staff and what helps them settle into a new placement or organisation. Using attachment theory, the authors look at how early and past experiences shape the children and young people's responses to transitions. The chapter discusses the new relationship-building needed when a child arrives, but also, the need to appreciate the child's loss of other important relationships. The latter part of the chapter looks at the importance of processes of staff induction and support.

In Chap. 4, Behaviour as Communication, Dave Roberts discusses the many ways in which behaviour communicates how children are feeling. He argues that behaviour often communicates a need that may be outside the child's awareness. As in other chapters, the emphasis is on relationship-building through sensitive understanding of what is behind a child's potentially challenging behaviour. The chapter explores why children may not be able to communicate their feelings verbally and why this can be almost as hard for adults when asked to engage in honest reflection. The 'Six Stages of Distress' model in introduced, alongside that of the 'Five R's'.

In Chap. 5, What to Do About Strong Feelings?, Siobhan Foster-Weston and Caryn Onions tease out the need for physical and emotional safety before exploring feelings. The chapter builds on the previous one, as once children show the behaviours which other settings have not been able to manage, therapeutic relationship-building can begin. The chapter develops the psychodynamic perspective further: not mean simply 'talking about feelings' and allowing children to do whatever they want. The chapter's focus is on how to tackle boundary-setting using therapeutic language and how to recognise that saying 'no' in various ways is still important. The chapter includes practice dilemmas where staff or carers and professionals have different views and different levels of tolerance about boundary-setting.

In Chap. 6, Working Things Out with Children and Families, Caryn Onions explores working with families using practice examples of group and individual work and staff supervision. The chapter focuses on therapeutic relationships to gain trust and deepen insight for families who feel stuck. The examples include understanding loss and the impact on people's individual and family lives. It focuses on listening to and fully taking in the feelings that each person brings to the situation, in order that the practitioner can tease out what is going on and why children, parents, and carers might be trapped in painful or unhelpful repetitive ways of being together.

In Chap. 7, Supporting Staff, Dave Roberts and Heather Price argue for better support for all staff doing the skilled, difficult and stressful work of caring and educating children with complex needs. The focus is on reflective practice that improves staff understanding the impact of the work on themselves and their practice. The chapter outlines the process of individual and group supervision at the Mulberry Bush. Practice examples containing real-life dilemmas are taken from a range of other different settings. The authors acknowledge that reflective practice focussing on the emotional impact of the work on oneself is a new form of support and supervision for many mainstream settings.

In Chap. 8, Keeping Children at the Heart of Collaborative Working, Mike Staines considers the importance of collaboration for how professionals work together in ways that are genuinely in the child's best interests. Using practice examples in a variety of settings, including the Mulberry Bush treatment team model with families and professional networks, it teases out the difficulties that can arise when people do not put the child's needs first. The chapter reviews why working together can be challenging, and some practical steps to bear in mind.

In Chap. 9, Leaving and Endings, Caryn Onions explores how we help children and staff say goodbye. It looks at theory around loss and separation and the feelings we all grapple with. Many of the children described in the book will have had sudden and upsetting leavings and will not have experienced a good, coherent and meaningful ending. The chapter includes what we have learnt from placement breakdowns and unplanned endings. The final section focuses on leaving care and shares what it was like for two care experienced adults accessing their care records.

In Chap. 10, Becoming Research Minded, Caryn Onions and Heather Price consider how practitioners and organisations can take seriously the role of empirical research. The chapter recognises different levels of involvement including reading and training, action research, implementing evidence-based schemes and working with external researchers. Using a variety of real case studies, the authors highlight different ways in which staff and organisations can make use of research and increase their research mindedness. The important element is always how this affects practice.

Finally, in Chap. 11, Concluding Thoughts, Caryn Onions, Heather Price and Dave Roberts bring together the main messages from the book. It starts with an overview from the authors that, in the UK, we need our education and care systems to shift focus towards a genuine relationship-based, inclusive approach. It reviews the overarching themes of the book, which include the emotional availability of the practitioner, and how this can be supported by embedding reflective supervision and practice into organisations, collaborative work and psychodynamic practice.

Throughout the book, we suggest that the reader takes time to 'pause for thought', to have focused moments to think about the issue being discussed in relation to their own setting.

References

Children's Commissioner. (2024). *Press notice: Over a quarter of a million children still waiting for mental health support, Children's Commissioner warns.* Retrieved July 30, 2025, from https://www.childrenscommissioner.gov.uk/blog/over-a-quarter-of-a-million-children-still-waiting-for-mental-health-support/

Department for Education. (2025). *Suspensions and permanent exclusions in England, Spring term 2023/24 - Explore education statistics.* Retrieved July 30, 2025, from https://explore-education-statistics.service.gov.uk/find-statistics/suspensions-and-permanent-exclusions-in-england/2023-24-spring-term

Institute for Government. (2023). *Performance tracker 2023: Children's social care.* Retrieved July 30, 2025, from https://www.instituteforgovernment.org.uk/publication/performance-tracker-2023/childrens-social-care

National Audit Office. (2024). *Support for children and young people with special educational needs.* Retrieved July 30, 2025, from https://www.nao.org.uk/reports/support-for-children-andyoung-people-with-special-educational-needs/

Stafford, J., Aurelio, M., & Shah, A. (2020). Improving access and flow within child and adolescent mental health services: A collaborative learning system approach. *BMJ Open Quality, 9*(4), Article e000832.

CHAPTER 2

Roots of the Mulberry Bush Approach

Heather Price and Caryn Onions

Introduction

Have you ever felt a profound sense of relief when a child you are expecting to work with, or care for, is not around that day?

Vignette 1

James is a teaching assistant in a mainstream secondary school. He's been supporting Poppy and several other pupils in her Year 7 class in core subjects this term. James finds it almost impossible to get Poppy to focus on her work. Unless he is very firm, she will distract him with loud, teasing questions about his likes, dislikes and personal life, sit overly close to him, and want to chat and share personal confidences. When he sets boundaries, she accuses him of disliking her and becomes sulky and then angry, often further disrupting the lesson. When James is supporting another pupil, Poppy will interrupt, calling out and demanding his attention. She frequently ends up sitting one to one with a member of staff in the 'inclusion room'.

C. Onions et al., *Supporting Children and Young People with Complex Needs*, Palgrave Texts in Counselling and Psychotherapy, https://doi.org/10.1007/978-3-032-16699-9_2

Pause for thought: Perhaps you have encountered children like Poppy in your work. How do you think Poppy makes James feel, and how would you feel about working alongside Poppy? Why do you think Poppy is behaving like this?

Poppy might make adults working alongside her feel uncomfortable, particularly male staff. She might also make teaching staff feel exasperated, or suffocated, or angry or helpless. It is difficult to know exactly why Poppy is behaving like this, and it can be hard to think clearly about a young person when they stir up such strong feelings. Staff may not always be told a great deal about a young person's background, although they might be informed if they have a specific learning difficulty such as dyslexia, or a diagnosis such as attention deficit hyperactivity disorder. Poppy clearly finds the work challenging. She seems to want exclusive adult attention in a setting where it is not available and demands that attention in a way that is inappropriate. It is hard to meet her needs, and she disrupts other children from learning.

Vignette 2

Paulette is a foster carer for Mo, aged seven, who has been excluded from his primary school for violent behaviour. Unlike James, Paulette has a good idea of why Mo is violent, particularly towards her, and why he tries to control every situation through domineering behaviour (this includes undermining other children's relationships with Paulette and with each other). From a young age, Mo witnessed domestic violence between his parents until his father was imprisoned for drug dealing. Mo has a history of being violent towards his birth mother, who was unable to keep him or herself safe.

Pause for thought: You might also have encountered children like Mo in your work, particularly if you work in the social care system. How would you feel if you were caring for Mo? How helpful would it be to know something of Mo's background?

Mo might make adults who are trying to parent him feel angry, intimidated and unsafe, particularly female carers. He might make his foster family feel as if they want to exclude him in the way his school has done. Knowing something about Mo's background might help Paulette to experience his attacks in a less personal way, to feel some compassion for him, and to reflect on whether he is perhaps copying his dad, or 'acting out' what he saw at home in his early years. However, knowing why Mo behaves as he does may not always help with how to best manage his behaviour or how to address the underlying causes of it.

We have opened this chapter with two vignettes we hope capture some common predicaments faced by staff and carers when working with children 'on the edge' of education and family life. Here, we are thinking about children in and on the edge of the care system, and children with complex social, emotional, mental health and disability needs whose anxiety and / or behaviour places them at particular risk of school exclusion. The chapter (and this book) is about ways of working with these difficulties that have been developed at the Mulberry Bush School. The school's approach has been applied in outreach work with mainstream schools and alternative provision, with social workers, in social care settings in foster, adoptive and children's homes, and with young people in the criminal justice system.

In what follows, we introduce three key principles informing work undertaken by the Mulberry Bush. As noted in the introduction, the Mulberry Bush is a seventy-five-year-old charity with a focus on specialist therapeutic provision for children, young people and families affected by childhood trauma. Many of the children and young people helped by the Mulberry Bush have high numbers of adverse childhood experiences (ACEs) in their backgrounds, impacting their thinking, relating and behaviour. A significant number also have attendant diagnoses such as attention deficit disorder or conduct disorder, and many are neurodiverse. As a therapeutic community, the core aims of the Mulberry Bush have always been to foreground a compassionate, therapeutic stance towards the children's difficulties, to be curious about them, and for everyone to be able to draw on support from across the community in coping with work (and life) alongside each other.

The latter part of this chapter looks at two key theoretical ideas developed by the charity's founder, Barbara Dockar-Drysdale, in the 1950s and 1960s. Although these were written around sixty years ago, we argue they are still as relevant today as they were when the charity was first founded.

Chapter Aims

By introducing the charity's three principles, and some core theoretical ideas, this chapter

- Demonstrates what it means to work therapeutically when one is not a therapist;
- Provides insight into the thinking and reflection that practitioners can do individually and in teams to help with the work;
- Shows how practitioners can look under the surface of what might be going on with children, young people, and in teams;
- Focuses on the process that staff go through to understand the impact on them individually of undertaking therapeutic work;
- Supports practitioners in a range of diverse settings.

Practice-Based Principles

Three practice-based principles underpin the work of the Mulberry Bush. These are psychodynamic practice, collaborative working, and reflective practice. The following practice dilemmas illustrate how we understand the work using these principles (Fig. 2.1).

'Getting under the surface' Using a Psychodynamic Approach

Experience has shown that if we are able to understand why someone is behaving in a certain way, and particularly if the behaviour is distressing to those around them, we are more likely to have empathy and to help them find a way through.

What do we mean by the term 'psychodynamic approach'? The phrase 'getting under the surface' describes the essential quality of the psychodynamic approach. It does not take things at face value but instead looks for deeper hidden meanings. In this book we highlight the importance of unconscious parts of the mind, those outside our awareness.

> ...where there is a lively relationship between different aspects of the personality, formed through past and present relationships between the growing individual and significant others, and therefore consciously and unconsciously influencing relationships with the 'internal world' of the mind, and with the external world of persons and objects. (Jacobs, 1991, p. xii)

In the early 1970s, Barbara Dockar-Drysdale wrote about staff trying to get 'under the surface' of the children's behaviour.

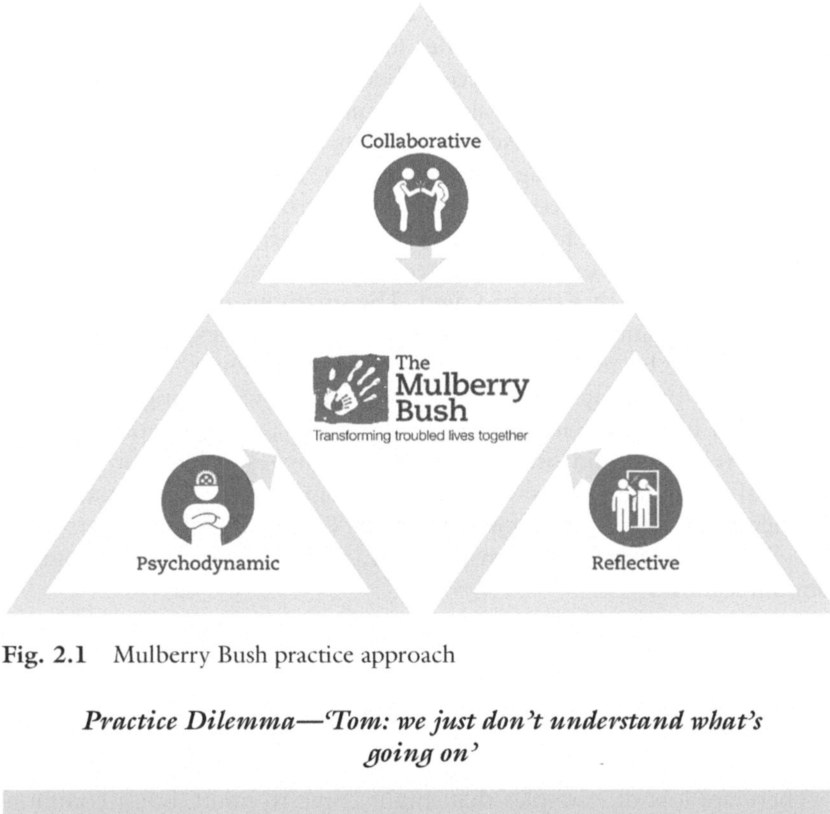

Fig. 2.1 Mulberry Bush practice approach

Practice Dilemma—'Tom: we just don't understand what's going on'

A boy, Tom, aged nine, at the Mulberry Bush some years ago broke windows for no apparent cause, and with tremendous violence. It was finally possible to link these explosions with a breakdown in communication with his mother. When this happened—when no letter arrived—Tom became convinced that she was dead. Waiting for the news of her death produced tension and panic so terrific that the smashing of glass produced temporary relief (Dockar-Drysdale, 1973, p. 127).

This type of dangerous behaviour, which puts people at risk, can easily create panic and fear in staff, children and young people. In some organisations it could lead to staff making knee-jerk decisions, perhaps sanctions and punitive solutions, which fit less comfortably alongside a therapeutic approach. Piecing the story together in the example above, it sounds as though staff had to experience Tom's behaviour several times before colleagues came together to think about the meaning of the smashed glass for Tom. Staff were able to unpack the feelings that Tom repeatedly experienced when hearing nothing from his mother. It might have been easy to assume that Tom smashed windows only out of anger, but we get the impression that waiting for his mother's letter to arrive became unbearable for him, and that his explosions of feeling were not just out of fury with his mother but fear that she had died. The smashing also meant Tom was trying to take some control, albeit in a violent and destructive way. He could not make his mother communicate or send a letter, but he found a powerful way of letting staff know that something was wrong.

Fear that his mother might have died is quite a different concept from anger or rebellion, and one that needs and invites a different response from staff. Communication between staff, and between staff and Tom, will inevitably have been important to help Tom when future letters were due. We will return to this in Chap. 4, which looks at 'behaviour as communication'.

> *Pause for thought:* Can you think of a time when you realised afterwards what someone's behaviour might have meant?

There are lots of examples that might come to mind, but a common one is where a child or young person pushes you away aggressively. While the overt meaning might be that they want you to 'leave them alone', there is often a testing out to see if you will in fact abandon them to their feelings, rather than helping in some way.

Collaborative Working

There are often many professionals working with a child or young person at the same time. They will each have their own perspective informed by their training and experience of the situation. So how do they come together and find a way forward that takes account of these differences? Seikkula and Arnkil (2006) argue that the aim of the professionals' conversations is not.

> unanimous understanding of the problem as the basis of a plan for action. The point of departure is, on the contrary, that each person has his/her own specific view on the matter. It is important to try to understand each point of view. The new understanding is created at the boundary of the parties, as no one person's point of view takes precedence. (Seikkula & Arnkil, 2006, p. 91)

At the core of this collaborative approach is respect that everyone's voice be heard. This approach is based on family therapy, where the key idea is that therapists join families rather than focus on and interpret their interactions.

Practice Dilemma: 'trying to make sense without the full story'

An 8-year-old girl, recently looked after, was reported as behaving inappropriately at school. Among other unusual behaviours, she was refusing to come out from under a table in certain lessons. In a meeting with the key adult network, the social worker explained the current conditions of her life, that she had not seen her mother for some time and had no knowledge of what was happening in her family. It can be difficult to know what to say to children when care proceedings are pending and there is great uncertainty about the outcome. In the foster home she was very quiet and compliant. Thinking together, we were able to put together our knowledges of her and come to appreciate how she may be feeling, perhaps desperately worried about her mother and other family relationships, guilty and ashamed that she had 'broken' her family and determined to say nothing more in case she made it worse, fearing or knowing that she was 'bad' and it was 'all her fault' (Lobatto, 2021, p. 481).

New emerging understandings develop for colleagues as they listen to the perspective of others close to the child. They hold different pieces of the jigsaw puzzle and by sharing perspectives may come to a new shared view of the child's situation. The hope is that network meetings like this can bring new depths to collaboration where individuals feel heard.

Bringing together different professional views can also reduce the feelings of isolation that people often hold yet do not share. Children and young people on the edge of school and family life will knowingly/consciously and unknowingly/unconsciously communicate their anxiety, which those close to them will pick up.

Pause for thought: This network of professionals shared their knowledge of the girl and came up with different ways of understanding her 'under the table' behaviour. Are you in a similar situation in your workplace?

It can be important to be aware of how supportive and accessible you experience your team, organisation and wider collaborative network. Carrying out a quick mental inventory of the formal and informal 'ports of call' available to you can help you appreciate where there might be support or resources you are under-utilising, but also to note where you find support to be inadequate. Collaborative working is discussed in more depth in Chap. 8.

Reflective Practice

The Health and Care Professions Council (HCPC) defines reflection as 'a process which helps you gain insight into your professional practice by thinking analytically about any element of it' (HCPC, 2021). It involves talking and thinking with colleagues about all aspects of the work. It is more than ad hoc conversations, routine meetings and supervision. 'Lara' was a participant in a research project looking at reflective practice at the Mulberry Bush; she gives a childcare worker's view of it in the extract below.

Practice Dilemma—Going Round in Circles

'Lara', a new Therapeutic Care Practitioner, reported that initially she found the reflective milieu a load of mumbo jumbo crap but gradually came to value it, describing previous work in another children's home without it: 'it was like firefighting all the time. You didn't have any support from anywhere else. For inexperienced staff that was really dangerous because they didn't understand the process of the work. Lots of people ended up leaving because they couldn't cope. I think it definitely affected other people's mental health because they didn't feel able to speak up about it, they were worried they'd lose their jobs' (Price et al., 2023, p. 12).

Lara had worked in another children's home before coming to the Mulberry Bush but had found it difficult to manage the emotional load of the young people. In the research interview, she described how she loved working with children, but it felt too 'dangerous' as the staff were not encouraged to talk about any of these emotional aspects and how it left them feeling. When she started at the Mulberry Bush, she had the same overwhelming feelings, especially in relation to Ellie, her key child, and she began to think there was something wrong with her own mental health. Lara felt increasingly 'useless and isolated'. Her manager suggested she take her feelings to group supervision 'which was both terrifying and a relief'. The team helped Lara think about what Ellie might be replaying from her past. They helped her slowly tease out how Ellie's early experiences were what Lara was struggling to understand. Wondering 'who the feelings belong to' takes a while to work out and is often an experience that people have when working therapeutically.

The reflective supervision provided the support that Lara needed to begin to understand the emotional aspects of the work. By sharing their experiences of working like this, Lara's colleagues described how staff need time to process these emotional aspects of the work. This is slow work, and may feel very uncomfortable at the start for some people.

Studies have shown that providing a reflective milieu and encouraging staff to share practice, including the challenges, can lead to stronger and more cohesive teams. Undertaking emotionally demanding work is supported by having trusted colleagues, and in turn, staff retention and sickness absence are also improved (Tham, 2022; Steinkopf et al., 2021). Reflective group discussions have also been shown to help practitioners critically consider their bias and other influences on the work, as well as helping them hold back their own views to better consider others. They can also help staff manage uncertainty (Julien-Chinn & Lietz, 2019). Finally, reflective practice is thought to help practitioners persevere with challenging cases and develop a better understanding of the meaning of individual and family behaviour (Lees, 2017).

Pause for thought: Do you reflect on your work with colleagues? If so, how do you think it affects your practice? If not, how might you suggest to colleagues that you introduce this in your setting?

It can be challenging to suggest the need for reflective supervision with colleagues. Jonathan Willis (2017), a Deputy Head Teacher at a Social and Emotional Mental Health (SEMH) Special School, raised the need for a group with his senior leadership team after a training day designed to address low morale in his school. In Chap. 7, you can read about what happened when the school introduced reflective supervision.

The three principles above support staff and carers in sustaining an interest in the less obvious meanings behind a person's behaviour, in working together in as democratic a way as possible to share ideas about a difficulty, and in bearing the emotional load associated with applied therapeutic work.

The second half of this chapter explores two core theoretical ideas developed by the Mulberry Bush's founder, Barbara Dockar-Drysdale. These are 'the provision of primary experience' and 'the management of violence'. We will argue that these two concepts, which are more than sixty years old, can still speak to the needs of children like Poppy, Mo and Tom, and of staff like James, Paulette and Lara, who are working alongside them.

Lessons from History

The Provision of Primary Experience

Barbara Dockar-Drysdale was one of the first psychologists to argue that many children on the edge of education and family life draw attention to their needs through their behaviour, and this need for focused attention is legitimate. They need a caring adult open to their states of mind, who, she said, will 'feel and act like a mother with her new-born baby...with the same preoccupation and sense of vulnerability' (quoted in Reeves, 2002, p. 10). She called this 'the provision of primary experience' (Dockar-Drysdale, 1991).

In the 1940s and 1950s, the Mulberry Bush was originally taking care of children who had been evacuated from cities during the Second World War. Some of these presented as 'delinquent' and were from 'deprived' households. As time went on, the school developed a reputation for taking these 'difficult' children. Initially, Dockar-Drysdale argued that deprived and neglected children should be allowed to 'regress' and have their needs met at a level that was below their chronological age. So, for example, warm milk and rusks were given to children aged ten or twelve years old, alongside special one-to-one attention at bedtime, as if they were still in their early years and somehow 'frozen' in their development. Dockar-Drysdale felt there was a need to accept they could not yet move on, and it was not helpful to pressure them to do so.

The idea that children who 'act out' have been neglected or abused by their parents and others is now fairly commonplace, and as some feminists have pointed out, it can be used as a stick to beat parents with, especially mothers (Riley, 1983). But many children and young people have been deprived of what they need and needed, for many different psychosocial reasons, lots of them beyond their parents' control. The idea that such children might need an adult's full attention for some time is now accepted in various forms of relational therapeutic parenting (Hughes & Baylin, 2012; Bombèr & Perry, 2020) but is less accepted in educational settings and in children's homes for young people, where teens may present as if they are older than their years, and apparently not in need of 'babying'.

Today, trauma-informed and trauma-focused work with children and young people recognises the need for those affected to be closely attended to and understood at a deep personal level. It is accepted that they may not present at a level of personal development or maturity commensurate with their chronological age. Where there has been loss of primary safety, of recognition of the reality of a person's needs and experience, and of connection to trusted others, trust and growth will take time. Judith Hermann's (1992) highly influential trauma-informed model notes that the path to hope, re-engagement with life and post-traumatic growth involves recovering safety, unpicking of the denial of the losses and damage inflicted by trauma, and restoration of social connections. Supporting this work is through building one-to-one relationships and is very like the work of early parenting. Like early parenting, it is very demanding.

An early pupil at the Mulberry Bush, attending in the 1950s, reflected on her experience of what Barbara Dockar-Drysdale would have labelled 'the provision of primary experience':

'Sally', at the Mulberry Bush in the 1950s

'I recall two teachers in particular who I started to trust there. There is one incident that I remember very clearly. I dug this huge hole in the ground, and I found some corrugated iron, and I put it over this hole and just left an opening to get into it. And that was my kind of den if you like, and I was allowed to do it! Health and safety nowadays wouldn't… And I invited these three teachers into my den, and they actually came, and they actually crawled in. And it must have been incredibly hard for them, and they crawled into my den, and they sat there with me. And I think that was the outstanding moment when I felt okay and that they accepted me for me.'

Pause for thought: Imagine that poppy has a place at one of the (rare) mainstream secondary schools that has a nurture group system, and she elects to attend it regularly. And Mo's foster mother, Paulette, has had higher-level training, to be able to offer a specialist 'therapeutic' foster placement. Do you think this will make a difference for poppy and Mo?

We can note that these interventions might help, but for quite a long time, children and young people can also seem unable to make use of what caring adults and peers offer them, particularly if other areas of their lives are not safe or stable. Therapeutic educating and caring, providing a 'primary experience' of attuned attention, may need very hard work for a long time. Staff and carers are therefore likely to feel frustrated, and this can lead to feelings of anger, despair and rejection—a 'why bother' experience of compassion fatigue that speaks very directly to the need for staff support, as noted above.

The Management of Violence

Attachment theory (Howe & Betts, 2023) has shed light on the ways in which children and young people who have experienced trauma may reject the attuned care offered to them, repeating instead more compliant or controlling and demanding styles of relating that have served them well in their past traumatising relationships. Contemporary neuroscience and theories that look at traumatised children's struggles to 'mentalize' (Midgley & Vrouva, 2012) can now help us to understand the less mature thought processes and extreme emotions that accompany dysregulated children's interpersonal styles of relating, and their potential for extreme 'acting out'. Donovan and Kingswood (2023) acknowledge it is uncomfortable to attribute violence and intent to harm to children, but there is now an increasing amount of research on, for example, child to parent violence (Baker & Bonnick, 2021) and the increased risk of childhood victims of violence becoming perpetrators or being involved in the criminal justice system (Mbilinyi et al., 2012).

The term 'dysregulation' or even 'meltdown' does not capture the sense of intimidation that children's and young people's violent acts and words can induce in parents, carers and other professionals. 'Michelle', another participant in the research project on reflective practice at the Mulberry Bush, applied to work as a teaching assistant there and was invited to spend a day at the school before deciding to continue with her application. She commented, '*It said something like "emotionally troubled children" on the advert, and I think in my mind that meant children would be emotional in the sense of tearful and very sensitive… It was quite – the day I visited was quite – it was like a traumatic day in class* [there were several violent peer-on-peer and child-to-adult incidents and consequent restraints]. *When I got the job they said oh some people don't even turn up to the interview after they've visited! And I was like wow, okay, I can see why.*' Later she added in her interview, '*For me the children that get under my skin … are children that make me anxious … I mean really anxious in terms of like a sick feeling*' (adapted from Price et al., 2017, p. 133).

Many children originally sent to the Mulberry Bush in the 1950s to 1970s were placed there because they were felt to be 'unmanageable' or 'beyond parental control', and this remains the case today. One of Barbara Dockar-Drysdale's important but controversial insights was the claim that 'babies who have not had enough primary experience from their mothers experience helpless rage' (Dockar-Drysdale, 1991, p. 139). Children and young people who have experienced trauma carry not just fear but rage at what has happened to them. They often cannot think or speak about their experiences, for a range of reasons, and convey them through their behaviour, particularly their violent and abusive actions towards other people.

In a 70th anniversary book of the work of the Mulberry Bush (Diamond, 2018), John Diamond, then the charity's Chief Executive Officer, commented: 'Staff support each other by both remembering that within an aggressor there is always a victim, and that the act of violence is a direct enactment and communication of the child's unbearable feeling, in order to pass it on and make the other feel what it is like to be abused, abandoned and hurt' (Diamond, 2018, pp. 15–16).

Dockar-Drysdale (1991, p. 133) argued that what is unmanageable for the child or young person has to be managed by staff. She outlined four key principles for managing violence:

- accepting responsibility for keeping lines of communication open (with the children and with other members of the community).
- knowing one's own violent feelings so one doesn't act out in turn.
- supporting verbal or other safe means of communicating violent feelings.
- taking responsibility for protecting children and their peers from the consequences of violence.

These principles, defined very early on, attempted to keep the Mulberry Bush workplace and home safe for everyone. They foreshadow contemporary trauma-focused ways of working: maintaining a sense of safety, communicating about damage and loss rather than denying them or 'turning a blind eye', and sustaining social connections with others (Strand & Sprang, 2018).

Pause for thought: Have you witnessed or been on the receiving end of violence (physical or verbal) from a child or young person in the course of your work? What procedures and sources of support are available for you, as a professional, in your setting? Do they link in any way to the four points above?

Your answers to these questions might prompt you to reflect on the need for 'debriefs' and one-to-one supervisory support for purposes of self-care after difficult encounters, as well as regular supervisory or support spaces where carers and workers can regularly 'put' their feelings.

In thinking about violent 'acting out', 'Sally', one of the original pupils at the Mulberry Bush whom we quoted above, described her experience of trying to put into practice some of the 'ways of being' she had been shown.

'Sally', talking about life after leaving the Mulberry Bush in the late 1950s

'When I'd started out on life with nothing, actually one of the things I learned from being at the Bush was to communicate, because I was never really able to communicate with people. When I left school and finished up scrubbing floors, I sort of thought about it. As I scrubbed away, I was actually using energy, something I had also learned at the Bush – it reduced my level of frustration. I thought, Sally, you're not gonna live your life doing this. I was very angry and when I talked to Dr Kerry (who played a big part in my going to the Bush in the first place) she was, "What did you do at the Bush then?" "They helped me deal with my anger." "You didn't go smashing up fences or beating someone in the face or something did you, what did you do?" And she reminded me of the things I had learned just spontaneously and through the example of the staff and the team and their tolerance, that yeah, it's in my hands. I took the bull by the horns and left the job. [At the Bush was] when I really learned that ability to actually talk and not sit in the corner and cry or break things and throw things around… I do have bad moments…there's been many times in my life when I've had to stop and think wow, hang on here, and little triggers go back to the Bush.'

Conclusion

The approach of the Mulberry Bush has taken more than seventy-five years to develop. So much has changed over these years in the UK and internationally, especially in relation to how we think about the education, care and treatment of children who struggle to find their place in school and family life. We have introduced you to Dockar-Drysdale's innovative ways of thinking about these children and young people and argued that this perspective is still relevant today. Perhaps a difference between practice now and in Dockar-Drysdale's time is our emphasis on relationships and 'relational practice' as the means to therapeutic change. It is implicit in what Dockar-Drysdale wrote, but nowadays we focus on it much more with staff, as will become evident in later chapters. The next chapter will focus on how we use this thinking when a child, young, person or adult is new in a setting.

References

Baker, V., & Bonnick, H. (2021). *Understanding CAPVA: A rapid literature review on child and adolescent to parent violence and abuse for the domestic abuse commissioner's office, respect.* Retrieved August 28, 2025, from CAPVA-Rapid-Literature-Review-Full-November-2021-Baker-and-Bonnick.pdf

Bombèr, L., & Perry, A. (2020). *Know me to teach me: Differentiated discipline for those recovering from adverse childhood experiences.* Worth Publishing.

Diamond, J. (2018). *70 years of the mulberry bush school: Showing the way in therapeutic childcare.* The Mulberry Bush School.

Dockar-Drysdale, B. (1973). *Consultation in child care.* Longman.

Dockar-Drysdale, B. (1991). *The provision of primary experience: Winnicottian work with children and adolescents.* Jason Aronson, Inc..

Donovan, S., & Kingswood, C. (2023). *The unofficial guide to therapeutic parenting for childhood aggression and violence.* Jessica Kingsley Publishers.

Health and Care Professions Council. (2021). 'What is reflection?'. Available at: What is reflection? | The HCPC. Retrieved May 27, 2025, from Hcpc-uk.org/standards/meeting-our-standards/reflective-practice/what-is-reflection/

Hermann, J. (1992). *Trauma and recovery: The aftermath of violence—From domestic abuse to political terror.* Basic Books.

Howe, D., & Betts, L. R. (2023). *Attachment across the Lifecourse: A brief introduction.* Bloomsbury Academic Press.

Hughes, D., & Baylin, J. (2012). *Brain-based parenting: The neuroscience of caregiving for healthy attachment.* W. W. Norton and Company.

Jacobs, M. (1991). *The presenting past.* Open University Press.

Julien-Chinn, F., & Lietz, C. (2019). Building learning cultures in the child welfare workforce. *Children and Youth Services Review, 99*, 360–365.

Lees, A. (2017). *Evaluation of reflective practice groups project: Brighton & Hove Children's services.* Centre for Social Work Practice.

Lobatto, W. (2021). Using systemic principles in the design of mental health and wellbeing services for looked after children and young people—Bringing together research, theory and practice. *Journal of Family Therapy, 43*(3), 469–488.

Mbilinyi, L. F., Logan-Greene, P. B., Neighbors, C., Walker, D. D., Roffman, R. A., & Zegree, J. (2012). Childhood domestic violence exposure among a community sample of adult perpetrators: What mediates the connection? *Journal of Aggression, Maltreatment & Trauma, 21*(2), 171–187.

Midgley, N., & Vrouva, I. (2012). *Minding the child: Mentalization-based interventions with children, young people and their families.* Routledge/Taylor & Francis Group.

Price, H., Brown, J., Herd, J., & Jones, D. (2023). 'A bit like you're going to therapy': Reflective practice provision at the Mulberry Bush School. *Residential Treatment for Children & Youth, 40*(4), 517–536.

Price, H., Herd, J., Jones, D., & Sampson, A. (2017). *'Keeping the children close': Towards an understanding of therapeutic provision at the mulberry bush school.* Retrieved May 27, 2025, from http://roar.uel.ac.UK/7089/1/UEL

Reeves, C. (2002). A necessary conjunction: Dockar-Drysdale and Winnicott. *Journal of Child Psychotherapy, 28*(1), 3–27.

Riley, D. (1983). *War in the nursery: Theories of the child and mother.* Virago.

Seikkula, J., & Arnkil, T. (2006). *Dialogical meetings in social networks.* Karnac.

Steinkopf, H., Nordanger, D., Halvorsen, A., Stige, B., & Milde, A. M. (2021). Prerequisites for maintaining emotion self-regulation in social work with traumatized adolescents: A qualitative study among social workers in a Norwegian residential care unit. *Residential Treatment for Children & Youth, 38*(4), 346–361.

Strand, V. C., & Sprang, G. (2018). *Trauma responsive child welfare systems.* Springer International.

Tham, P. (2022). Not rocket science: Implementing efforts to improve working conditions of social workers. *The British Journal of Social Work, 52*(4), 1896–1915.

CHAPTER 3

New Beginnings

Dawn Davidson and Siobhan Foster-Weston

Introduction

New beginnings, and the impressions they leave us with, can sometimes be etched on our memories. Or they can be so overwhelming that in retrospect, we remember little about them and nothing of how we were feeling at the time.

Vignette 1

Charlotte, aged eight, walks through the front door of the new school clutching her foster mum's hand. Her chin is tilted downwards, and she studiously avoids eye contact with the lady sitting behind the tall reception desk who is loudly and enthusiastically telling her how pleased she is to see her. A young man in a rainbow-coloured hoodie introduces

C. Onions et al., *Supporting Children and Young People with Complex Needs*, Palgrave Texts in Counselling and Psychotherapy, https://doi.org/10.1007/978-3-032-16699-9_3

himself as Joel and tells her that he is going to be her new Teaching Assistant and that she's going to love being in their class.

Pause for thought: Think back to the last time that you started a new job. Perhaps you were excited. Perhaps you were anxious. Perhaps you were dreading the enormity of the task of remembering people's names, what you were supposed to be doing and where you were supposed to be at any given time. You might have wondered about the new relationships you would have to form and whether there would be people in the new place who would resent your appointment. You might have worried about struggling to find your feet and fitting in.

Throughout childhood, children and young people are frequently asked to quickly acclimatise to new environments, to new people and to new expectations. On many occasions, the start of a new relationship means the loss of another. Starting anew is a daunting task for all of us, but potentially even more so for young people who have had turbulent beginnings to their lives. Carers may not have always been trustworthy or kind. Likewise, child-minders and teachers may have been insensitive to their needs. These considerations can help us to put in place more thoughtful processes that take into account the potential challenges for these young people.

The experience of joining a new setting for children who have experienced turbulent early years may feature many of the same thoughts and feelings you were asked about in the *Pause for thought*. The belief that love is all that is needed for children who have experienced turbulent early years is a well-meaning but simplistic view. These children are more likely to assume that they do not have the skills to find a place in a group, and that they are bound to fail.

In their 2021 paper, Gazilj, Borić and Cosić spoke to adolescents and caregivers about the feelings associated with the systems set up to help them. One foster carer commented:

> They don't trust adults. They've had no reason to trust adults from the beginning of their lives until now. When they come here, they don't see them as someone who wants to help them. Trust is earned. They are turned against the system, be it schools, be it social welfare, or be it the educational-correctional institution. I mean, throughout their lives they've had no reason to trust adults, their family and beyond. (Carer 1, Focus Group)

In new situations, many people have some sense of trust in others based on previous life experience, but this is often not the case for children and young people on the edge of school and family life. Consistency, predictability, and clear boundaries go some way to supporting a child to learn how to build the relationships that they will need in order to grow their capacity for trust. Often, the simple act of showing up, returning to work after a tricky interaction, or cooking a favourite meal after being on the receiving end of rude and rejecting behaviour, can be the key to helping the child to believe that things can be different. There is no short cut for the simple passage of time.

New settings can sometimes experience a 'honeymoon period' when a child joins. The initial settled period while the child finds their feet can lull carers into thinking that the child who has been described to them and the reports that they have read have been vastly exaggerated. It takes time for a child to learn to trust the people around them. If more challenging and anxiety-provoking behaviours emerge after this period, this might be both an indicator that the child feels safe enough to show their true self as well as the child testing the boundaries to see how these new people will respond. There might also be a splitting of behaviours in some situations, whereby the child presents very differently in one setting than another, such as in shared care, or between school and home. This might set up tensions or leave families wondering how they are getting it 'wrong'. It's important to note that for many children, being able to hold in their strong feelings to try to be 'good' is exhausting; something that can only be managed for a short time.

In this chapter we explore some of the ways in which practitioners can support children and young people to make successful transitions into new settings; for example, starting school for the first time, moving to a new foster carer or managing a transition to secondary school. We introduce some further ideas from attachment theory (which was discussed briefly in Chap. 2) to keep focussed on the importance of building relationships as a way of providing safety. Throughout the chapter we use examples from practice to highlight ways of thinking or responding that can be applied to a wide variety of new beginnings in a child or young person's life. We also consider new beginnings for staff and carers. We look at how putting systems in place to support new staff members can enable individuals to settle more easily within their teams and networks.

Chapter Aims

In this chapter we consider

- The feelings that children and young people might have in arriving in a new setting
- How early experiences might shape a child or a young person's reactions to transitions
- How practitioners might develop systems and processes to support new beginnings
- The mirroring of experience between adults and children
- What is helpful when bringing new team members into an organisation.

How Might We Apply Theory to Thinking About Beginnings?

Children who have experienced a world that is unpredictable, inconsistent, or frightening are likely to engage with new or unfamiliar adults as if they will also treat them in the same chaotic or even abusive way. John Bowlby, writing in 1969, described this as an internal working model; essentially a blueprint for how we relate to others, established in the early years. If a parent is warm, loving and responsive to our needs we develop a reciprocal view of ourselves as loveable and worthy of having our needs met. Conversely, a child who has been treated with hostility, neglect or inconsistent care may develop a sense of themselves as not deserving care and love, and adults as being unreliable or even punitive. Patricia Crittenden, whose extensive studies of parenting worldwide continue to inform our understanding of parent–child relationships, describes 'how stunningly competent … infants are at figuring out what you need to do to stay safe here, in this family where I was born, with these parents' (speaking with Marriott & Kelly, 2019).

In psychodynamic terms, 'transference' is the process by which a person relates to another as if they were a significant figure from their earlier life. A child who has experienced lack of consistency or unpredictability of response may relate to new, potentially supportive relationships with the same level of caution and self-protectiveness that would have been safe and necessary within the previous relationship, even if unnecessary and unhelpful in the new one. Staff may experience intense rejection or suspicion. This might result in the adult feeling rejected or struggling to connect with the child, sometimes to the extent that they may begin to question their capacity to do the work.

Vignette 2

Ty's early experience was marked by high levels of physical abuse by a father whose own childhood was marked by a parent who believed that 'sparing the rod spoiled the child'. Ty was regularly beaten for mistakes and even accidents such as spilling a drink or losing an item of school uniform. When he joined his foster family at the age of eleven, he had a deep mistrust of adults and would tell outrageous lies.

One day he came home from school with dripping wet shoes. In a concerned, parental way, his foster dad asked what had happened. Ty's eyes widened and he said, 'You'll never believe it, but I was walking past a puddle, and a huge wind came and blew the puddle right over my shoes!' It took many years of gentle responses, and loving and reliable shared problem-solving for him to believe that everyone makes mistakes and that he could safely tell the truth.

As early as 1944, John Bowlby observed that children who experience deprivation and abuse at the start of life struggle to form secure relationships. In addition, he noted that the outcomes for these youngsters were not as positive as those who had a secure and loving relationship with a consistent attachment figure (Bowlby, 1969). Contemporary research into the development of the brain bears out that abuse and neglect experienced in early childhood can negatively impact areas of the brain associated with emotional regulation and social behaviour (Putnam, 2006; Mueller & Tronick, 2019).

One of the key challenges for us when working with children with insecure attachment styles is that transitions can be particularly tricky. This includes daily transitions that seem insignificant, such as moving from waking to sleeping, or larger, more recognisable transitions such as a move to a new school. If a child has not received reliable and predictable care they may not have laid down the necessary experiences that allow them to cope easily with change. Questions such as 'Will you still be here when I get back?' or 'What if I'm not allowed to come back here if I leave?' might not be verbalised but might be acted out as heightened emotions such as distress, anger or resistance. This is discussed further in Chap. 4, Behaviour as Communication.

Supporting a child through transitions such as these can be physically exhausting for a carer as their sleep often becomes disrupted. It is important to ensure that self-care is factored in, as an exhausted carer or parent will find it harder to respond in thoughtful and attuned ways. The metaphor of the aeroplane oxygen mask is very pertinent: it's essential to first fit your own mask before you attempt to help others with theirs. Consideration of support networks, exercise and healthy eating are just as essential for the adult as for the child.

Donald Winnicott (1953) wrote about transitional objects after noticing how infants will assume that an object can act as a substitute for the mother in her absence. With older children and adolescents this may look different and may be initiated by the adults rather than the child. In many settings we have observed teachers and care workers using a form of transitional object to soothe a child's misgivings about the significant figure's absence and reassure them of reunion. For example, in one Alternative Provision, a gentle and intuitive secondary school teacher allowed her GCSE student to borrow her scarf while she was working with other students. It was a joy to see this otherwise tough and intimidating teenager studiously working at his desk with a colourful silk scarf wrapped around his neck.

Overlap to Avoid the Gap

Rather than wait until we encounter the non-verbal communications of anxiety and distress, experience suggests it is worth considering how we plan ahead for these transitions. Many schools arrange for their Year 6 students making the transition to secondary school to have planned visits in the half-term preceding the move. For children with complex needs we might wish to consider this form of provision, not only for the major moves, but for other transitions along the way. Things to be considered might include who would be the best person to support such visits and whether there is scope for relationship-building with significant adults ahead of the actual transfer. We might also think about the child's areas of strength so we can draw on these in order that the child is not coming solely from a position of deficit. Research has shown that the most positive outcomes occur when schools and families work together to support children to make the transition (Evangelou et al., 2008).

Vignette 3

Dean, a bright yet anxious nine-year-old, had struggled with impulse control, outbursts of aggression, and difficulties forming relationships with male teaching staff since Year 1. Now in Year 4, due to the attuned and thoughtful response of his school, he has managed to settle and, with the support of the class teaching assistant, is able to participate fully in class learning with only occasional outbursts. Recognising the step up in demand ahead of moving to Year 5, as well as the difficulties with building relationships with men, the school decided to arrange for Dean to play chess in the new classroom once a week during lunchtime with Mr. Tompkins, the Year 5 class teacher. By May half term, Dean has had numerous conversations with Mr. Tompkins as well as chances to see how his new teacher responds to both winning and losing at chess. He greets him warmly in the corridors and is less anxious about moving class.

Working with the child to find out what will help them to feel safe is immensely helpful. In residential or family settings, finding out what the child's favourite cartoon character or superhero is might mean that, when they arrive, their coat peg or bedroom door sign will feature something familiar. This shows that they have been held in mind prior to their arrival. Other considerations, such as knowing what their favourite cereal is or which brand of washing powder they are used to, might lend a sense of familiarity to the new setting.

While recognising the drive to avoid children feeling dropped, it is worth mentioning that there should also be space to support a child to mourn the loss of the previous relationship. Monica Lanyado (2002, p. 8) writes, 'Many authors have suggested that it is extremely difficult to mourn one relationship whilst trying to attach within another.'

As noted in the opening paragraph of this chapter, for many children, the start of a new relationship means the loss of another. However positive and hopeful the new setting might be, the child will have to come to terms with the fact that previous relationships will change. This is particularly pertinent in respect of fostering or adoptive care, where the child will be confronted with new parent figures and may encounter inner loyalty conflicts when recognising their growing feelings of warmth and attachment towards the new family. At times this can result in unexpected rejection just at the point when the new parent begins to feel that they are making progress and building a relationship.

Vignette 4

Patience, an experienced and skilful foster carer, describes feeling deskilled and hopeless when trying to form a relationship with her new foster child, Keeley. She tells the support group, 'I feel completely out of my depth. I've tried every tool in my box, and I've got nothing left'. The group wonders aloud whether what Patience is feeling might be similar to what Keeley is feeling. Patience reflects on everything that Keeley has been through in her fourteen years: six foster home breakdowns, a string of fixed-term exclusions followed by a permanent exclusion, and very irregular contact with her birth mum. Patience acknowledges that there seems to be a truth to this and says that she will hold this in mind next time she feels like she should give up.

If we consider that the feelings that we experience may mirror the feelings that our children are avoiding, it makes sense that children who are worried that however hard they try, they just won't get it right, might elicit similar feelings in the adults caring for them. Acknowledgement and acceptance of this can go some way to alleviate the guilt that the child might otherwise be left feeling. These are some of the reasons that reflective practice is so fundamental to this work. The ability to share such difficult feelings without fear of judgement or being shamed is important. It can enable new foster and adoptive carers, or residential staff members, to feel able to share their struggles and successes openly and honestly. This might feel quite counter-intuitive in a world where people often carefully curate how they present to the world. It may take time to feel comfortable with disclosure. Through appropriate provision of spaces to explore feelings as well as conscious modelling of owning our difficult feelings and mistakes, and being open about our own struggles, we create an environment where staff members can make good use of opportunities to work through complex feelings in the work.

The following quote, which is taken from a research project looking at reflective practice in a residential setting, summarises the lived experience of a new therapeutic childcare practitioner.

> For me, fear of being judged is very real and it takes a lot for me to ask for help and show people my own insecurities as well as acknowledging them myself. My supervisor helps me to share my experiences and feelings with the team. I am learning that I can't fix things on my own, and no one expects me to (Price et al., 2023, p. 9).

A Clean Sheet?

Pause for thought: Imagine that you go to see your doctor for a complaint that you have struggled with for years. Various forms of treatment have been trialled with varying levels of success. In your most recent consultation, your new GP says that he hasn't read your notes—he wants to come at it with a fresh pair of eyes. How do you feel about this?
Although this might be quite welcome, there is a potential danger that this new professional will try to reinvent the wheel or may even miss some key elements of your treatment that are essential to your well-being.

We might consider the same idea in relation to a child with complex needs. Children's records will include what we know of early experiences, interventions that have been tried, and conversations with the child and the wider network. Hopefully they will also contain some indication of the child's strengths, preferences, and what helps when they are finding things difficult. It is worth acknowledging that there may also be some unhelpful labels or generalisations but overall having some insight into the child's prior experiences and starting to make some sense of what this might mean for them will undoubtably be helpful. When considering behaviour as a communication, it is useful to think beyond the present predicament to what this might mean in the context of prior experience.

What About New Staff?

So far in this chapter we have focused on children's needs and how we might more successfully help them to settle into a new setting. In this section we will explore the process of staff induction in a residential care setting. Not all the processes described will be transferrable to other settings, and the process of preparation and training for foster and adoptive parents is necessarily different (and can take weeks if not months). The resources required from an organisation to prepare either group are significant. Sufficient preparation and support are particularly important in residential care, where employees may not have had any prior experience with children and young people on the edge of school and family life before becoming immediately responsible for them. It is crucial to get their support right, because recruitment of children's social care staff is an expensive process and maintaining good staff has benefits across the whole setting.

The following overview, written by a house manager at the Mulberry Bush School, details the thorough and careful process that has been developed to prepare new residential care staff for the task ahead.

> In our setting, recruitment is a thorough process involving a phone call, a visit, and a three-part interview. At all stages the emphasis is to be honest and open about the intensity of the work, digging into the challenges staff can face, as well as the resilience and support needed. Staff are encouraged to explore their own experiences that have led them to an interest in this type of work.

On arrival in the new setting, time is put aside to help staff to make sense of their role in the team, and their team in the wider organisation. This offers staff an insight into the structures that hold the organisation together.

Following a two-day cross-charity induction experience, new staff members participate in weekly breakfast meetings with other new staff facilitated by established leaders. It is a chance to revisit key information topics (Who should I go to when I need help with …? Where do I find …?, What do we mean by …?) that might otherwise be forgotten in the cognitive overload of the first few days. This is in addition to sharing systems and processes, routines and unfamiliar terminology.

Understandably, new staff tend to focus on the need for practical knowledge about their role. However, as time goes on and they start to feel the impact of building intense and sometimes painful relationships with the children, they will seek support to make sense of this. Initially, new staff are likely to benefit from informal structures such as peer support, especially from other new staff, where their feelings can be validated. The Mulberry Bush also has a system where new residential staff are allocated a mentor. The role of the mentor is to support with more day-to-day and practical elements of the role, holding new team members to time frames for undertaking or familiarising themselves with core tasks. This leaves space and time in supervision for the emotional impact of working with the children to be explored. This provides an opportunity for peer support, sharing of experiences, normalising feelings and recognising vulnerabilities. It also offers a space to explore what may make us vulnerable and how we manage those feelings in a contained way.

> *Pause for thought:* What does induction look like in your setting? Bearing in mind that high staff turnover can have a detrimental effect on the children as well as unsettling team dynamics, how can we use the skills and tools available to us to recruit and retain good team members?

One essential element of bringing a new staff member into the organisation is the availability of high-quality reflective supervision. Research shows that supervision reduces burnout (Iosim et al., 2021) and staff turnover (Chen & Scannapieco, 2010). It is vital that a trusting and honest relationship builds over time to allow the supervisee to feel comfortable enough to be open and, at times, vulnerable. The supervisor/supervisee relationship allows the supervisor to gain a good understanding of the supervisee's strengths and weaknesses (Chami-Malaeb, 2022). It is important to find the balance between protecting new staff from the feelings that can land with them and allowing staff to build up a resilience so that the children feel that staff can hold them emotionally. The children will often test new staff to see if they have the capability to keep them safe, and this can be challenging for them.

Interestingly, a common issue relates to new staff comparing themselves to their peers. Often feelings of frustration and envy are expressed. It is common to hear staff wonder 'why do the children listen and do what they've been asked to do by X but seem to ignore me?' Very quickly, both new staff and new children differentiate between those who can confidently manage a group and those who cannot. New staff may need to learn how different skills can be valued and how to manage their own expectations. A key element of supervision is helping new staff to understand that it requires self-reflection, openness and time to develop authority within the child group.

In addition to simply 'filling a vacancy', new staff members can offer something significant in terms of helping us to see our work with a new pair of eyes. We can encourage new members of staff to challenge existing structures. Are they free to question and be curious about what they are being asked to do? Can they ask what they might assume to be 'silly' questions and share with us any thoughts that they might have about the way that we function? Being open to this gives us an opportunity to reassess the reasons why structures and processes have been put in place. From time to time, something that was implemented at a particular time and for a certain reason may no longer be relevant. Equally, this might also be an opportunity for us to more clearly articulate our thinking and clarify practice. The following quote from a leader involved in bringing new staff into a care setting says:

> I often speak about the "fog" that seems to surround everything when you are new. Little, if anything, appears clear or straightforward. Unfamiliar processes and ways of working that initially do not make sense can feel alien and unclear. The desire for the concrete, the need to rely on rules and sanctions to manage your own anxieties, is high. Slowly, over time, this fog lifts and things start to make sense. As experiences are repeated, knowledge grows, and new staff begin to feel empowered.

Conclusion

This chapter explores the importance of preparing as carefully as we can for new beginnings for both children and adults. We need to think carefully about how things can be put in place to maximise success in a new setting even before the child arrives. Working alongside the child, understanding their behaviour as a communication and responding in thoughtful and empathic ways may help to break the negative narrative that they have built throughout their lives. Developing systems to support new staff will give us the best chance of reducing the loss of good people from the profession. The next chapter explores further how we understand the meaning of children's behaviour and what it communicates.

References

Bowlby, J. (1969). *Attachment and loss (No. 79)*. Random House.

Chami-Malaeb, R. (2022). Relationship of perceived supervisor support, self-efficacy and turnover intention, the mediating role of burnout. *Personnel Review, 51*(3), 1003–1019.

Chen, S.-Y., & Scannapieco, M. (2010). The influence of job satisfaction on child welfare workers' desire to stay: An examination of the interaction effect of self-efficacy and supportive supervision. *Children and Youth Services Review, 32*(4), 482–486.

Evangelou, M., Taggart, B., Sylva, K., Melhuish, E. C., Sammons, P., & Siraj-Blatchford, I. (2008). *What makes a successful transition from primary to secondary school?* Institute of Education https://discover.ucl.ac.uk/id/eprint/10005267/1/Taggart2008Whatmakesasucessful1.pdf

Gazilj, I., Borić, I., & Ćosić, A. (2021). The experience of residential care from the perspective of adolescents and caregivers. *Revija za elementarno izobraževanje, 14*(special), 35–61.

Iosim, I., Runcan, P., Dan, V., Nadolu, B., Runcan, R., & Petrescu, M. (2021). The role of supervision in preventing burnout among professionals working with people in difficulty. *International Journal of Environmental Research and Public Health, 19*(1), 160–175.

Lanyado, M. (2002). Creating transitions in the lives of children suffering from multiple traumatic losses. In L. Caldwell (Ed.), *The elusive child*. Karnac.

Marriott, S., & Kelly, A. (Hosts) (2019, May 15). Treating attachment & self-protective strategies with guest Patricia Crittenden (Part 1) (No. 96) [Audio podcast episode] In Therapist Uncensored Podcast. https://therapistuncensored.com/episodes/tu96-treating-attachment-self-protective-strategies-with-guest-patricia-crittenden-part-1/

Mueller, I., & Tronick, E. (2019). Early life exposure to violence: Developmental consequences on brain and behavior. *Frontiers in Behavioral Neuroscience*. ProQuest, https://www.proquest.com/scholarly-journals/early-life-exposure-violence-developmental/docview/2299766258/se-2

Munford, R. (2022). Children and young people in the care system: Relational practice in working with transitions and challenges. *Australian Social Work, 75*(1), 1–4.

Price, H., Brown, J., Herd, J., & Jones, D. (2023). 'A bit like you're going to therapy': Reflective practice provision at the Mulberry Bush School. *Residential Treatment for Children & Youth, 40*(4), 517–536.

Putnam, F. W. (2006). The impact of trauma on child development. *Juvenile & Family Court Journal, 57*(1), 1–11.

Winnicott, D. W. (1953). Transitional objects and transitional phenomena: A study of the first not-me possession. In L. Caldwell & H. Taylor Robinson (Eds.) 2016.*The collected works of D.W. Winnicott* (Vol. 4). Oxford University Press.

CHAPTER 4

Behaviour as Communication

Dave Roberts

'When a flower doesn't bloom, you fix the environment in which it grows, not the flower.'
—Alexander *Den Heijer (2018, p. 22)*

Introduction

When we think about communication, most of us would think about how something is expressed verbally, through writing or perhaps pictures or symbols. But while research, of course, recognises the importance of these different ways of communicating, actually, much of our communication occurs through our behaviour, which is heavily influenced by our relationships, our feelings and the environment around us. This means that, despite all the behaviour guides and training packages available for practitioners, understanding and responding to behaviour appropriately is not an exact science where a certain behaviour always has the same meaning. Instead, behaviour has many variables, which leaves workers with their own feelings and questions. Have you ever wondered why a child exhibits a certain behaviour or thought about the best way to respond? Have you ever wondered why a behaviour might be exhibited or whether the same behaviour is experienced by others?

C. Onions et al., *Supporting Children and Young People with Complex Needs*, Palgrave Texts in Counselling and Psychotherapy,
https://doi.org/10.1007/978-3-032-16699-9_4

Practice Example 1

Recently one of the Mulberry Bush Outreach team was asked to visit and support a local mainstream primary school who were finding the behaviour of a seven-year-old boy, Aiden, challenging. He repeatedly ran in and out of the classroom, made noises so the teacher could not be heard, and his disruptions seemed like a magnet for the other children. They asked us what to do to make Aiden stop and re-engage with his class. Our initial response of 'well let's try and understand why Aiden's doing these things rather than just trying to stop them' was met with some exasperation from the staff team who, by now, were worn down and frustrated that all their attempts appeared to have had limited success. 'We just want him to stop so we can teach the rest of the class' a staff member told us.

Pause for thought: Perhaps this sounds familiar to you? What might be the value of thinking about the feelings beneath the behaviour and why the child is doing this?

Clearly, Aiden's behaviour was experienced as challenging, having an impact on the learning of others while making those around him, both staff and children, feel anxious. However, by simply 'stopping' the behaviour we would be failing to meet the need behind the behaviour, which would, most likely, come out in a different way, most likely through a different type of behaviour. The idea that behaviour is communicating a feeling linked to an unmet need can be like looking through a kaleidoscope, where every time you turn it or someone else looks, the picture appears to be different. Staff working with Aiden looked at several interpretations of his behaviour before one of the staff, who clearly had a strong relationship with him, shared that Aiden had very low self-esteem and couldn't bear hearing feedback about his work. The staff group wondered together about whether the noise and running in and out allowed Aiden to avoid having to hear any feedback. This change in thinking then allowed the staff to try different non-verbal strategies of feeding back to Aiden rather than just focusing on his behaviour.

Pause for thought: What might the above example be communicating?

As with the practice example, this chapter focuses on questioning our thinking and explores how children's behaviour can be understood as a communication of need. We start by understanding this developmentally appropriate process, then look at communication in relation to children and young people on the edge of school and family life. Using practice examples from different settings, we describe how we develop our own, and the child's, understanding of what is behind their behaviour and how, slowly, we can see change through the lens of our working relationships. This use of relationships to help make sense of behaviour will run throughout this and subsequent chapters. It is important to recognise that often the process is not quick or easy and can require patience as well as thoughtfulness.

Aims of the Chapter

- To explore the idea that behaviour can be a communication of a feeling or an unmet need
- To link the ideas behind children's behaviour and self-reflection, so we can understand the potential impact we have on children's behaviour and
- To outline how the reader can apply the concept to a range of children's settings using models such as Six Stages of Distress and the 5 Rs.

It has long been clear that much of human communication is through our behaviour. Just think of the infant who has no speech or words, yet can communicate their unmet needs such as hunger, tiredness or pleasure. When children experience a safe and predictable environment they learn how to communicate as part of growing up. This means their childhood experiences impact greatly on this developing ability. The role of adults, whether parents/carers or professionals, is to support the development of this ability by taking the child's feelings, emotions and behaviour and processing them before giving them back to the child in a safe and presentable manner—like a parent, or carer, with a young baby.

When we think about behaviour as communication it is tempting to think that this refers to extreme behaviours, perhaps aggression or damage to property, but it applies to all types of behaviour, at all ages. For example:

1. Daisy, aged eight, will not let you go at bedtime—'*just one more story/drink/tuck in*'.

2. Fourteen-year-old Bailey's classwork suggests they put in minimum effort despite being academically able.
3. Louise, an experienced staff member, tends to avoid endings—perhaps a task or saying goodbye to others.

Before we consider these three examples, it is important to recognise that there is no right or wrong answer. When faced with behaviours that challenge us, we often want a clear answer or outcome because this helps contain our anxieties around the situation. However, our job is to help understand what is happening, using our intuition and hopefully our relationship with the child. It is the relationships that will provide the underpinning sense of security and trust for the child to build upon. Interventions on their own will have limited impact without connection and relationships. Interpreting behaviours without the context can be difficult and probably of limited value. What we want to get to is 'why does this child or young person keep doing this behaviour at this time?'

Let us think about what we know about the child who finds it hard to let you go, in Example 1. Perhaps the idea of being left with their own thoughts and feelings and the loss of your containing presence is too much: 'please don't leave me alone with these worries'. For a small number of children who have experienced night-time abuse, the feeling might be that further abuse might occur if you leave.

In Example 2, we see a child who appears to put in minimal effort or perhaps is bored or not feeing academically challenged. But what are the possible feelings behind this behaviour? Perhaps the child is worried about doing well and then being given even harder work or being separated from friends and moved to a 'top set'. Or perhaps the child feels that it is better not to try and fail than to have tried and to still fail, such is their fear of getting things wrong. Can we imagine living with those feelings? We must also bear in mind that the child might not know why they do not put in full effort.

Example 3 is probably a scenario many of us are familiar with and certainly overlaps with the first. Many of us avoid endings in different ways, and it is not unusual to see children finding it hard to finish an activity, come back in from break, put things away or say goodbye to someone. So, what is happening? Perhaps, at an unconscious level, there is a fear that a significant person will never return. Perhaps they have experiences of people abandoning them, or they avoid feeling the pain that comes with saying goodbye. Or maybe their apparent refusal to finish a task is because it feels safer to continue with a task they are familiar with and terrifying to have to move on and start something new.

What do we mean by Behaviour as Communication?

Through our interactions with others, and the ways in which we act, we communicate how we are feeling. Sometimes we are aware of it, and it is conscious; for example, when we avoid a situation that makes us anxious by pretending that we have something else more important to do. However, more often, we are not fully, if at all, aware of what we communicate, so it is unconscious. For example, without thinking, we might avoid spending time with someone because of the feelings this might arouse in us.

The ideas within this chapter are primarily related to these unconscious behaviours, or our 'out of awareness' behaviours, and psychodynamic ideas of getting under the surface. In Chap. 2 we highlighted the unconscious as referring to underlying thoughts and feelings that we are unaware of, but that influence and drive our behaviours (Jacobs, 2012). Much of our unconscious is formed through our childhood experiences, in utero and infancy, and what we observe from adults and, particularly for adolescents, from peers.

For a child who has experienced interpersonal early life trauma and possibly emotional neglect they may not have had a caregiver who could mentalise mentalize their experience (Fonagy & Target, 2003). What is significant is that if a child does not have a caregiver who can help them understand their feelings and reflect their true self back to them, then they do not develop the capacity to think about their own feelings and behaviour. If we consider the unconscious and accept that children may not be aware of what they are doing then we must accept they are even less likely to be able to look closely at their behaviour and understand why they behave in this way. As staff, this needs to make us question whether our expectations of children to stop or change behaviours are appropriate, or whether we are setting up the child to fail.

Practice Example 2

Chris was a senior care worker in a small, five-bedded, short-stay children's home for adolescents. Through supervisions and informal discussions, Chris often spoke about feeling overwhelmed by the work, going home feeling deflated and that the young people rejected his offers of support, activities or even conversation. This sense of rejection was recognised as a barrier that the young people built around themselves as relationships with Chris and other staff felt too scary. Rather than risk building a relationship that might be lost if they moved elsewhere, they unconsciously rejected everyone. For Chris, it was necessary, though painful, to experience the young people's feelings of rejection in order to recognise the meaning behind their communication.

At the Mulberry Bush, and other therapeutic settings, staff are supported to remain close to the children's feeling states, as well as their own (Price et al., 2018). This is achieved through a constant process of reflection, as discussed in Chap. 2, which helps staff recognise and consider their own feelings and explore what the children's behaviours might be communicating. This is how to make sense of what is happening with children and young people, but also, with ourselves.

Like Chris, those who work with children who exhibit behaviour that can challenge will recognise the enormous emotional impact of the work. The process of reflection and exploring behaviour as a communication is not only essential, but difficult and often painful. For example, staff may be more empathic and insightful if they have had their own experience of '*not wanting to go there*' with feelings and understanding their own behaviour, but it can still be extremely difficult, particularly if it is an unconscious block. It requires staff to be alongside a child, to develop a relationship and to experience, and be informed by the feelings, before staff can try to help make sense of the behaviour. This process takes time and is a way of working rather than a simple intervention. It is unlikely to happen in one interaction and may require a series of interactions, wonderings and apparent errors before any understanding is reached. The work takes time, and for many of us time is a valuable commodity that enriches the process of 'finding answers'.

Pause for thought: Think of a child/young person whose behaviour concerns you.
Consider: This box should be in the box above - I couldn't get it to copy above

Why can't they just say what's wrong? The link between thoughts and feelings

Frequently, behaviour is a sign that a child or young person may not have the necessary skills to tell you what they need to be emotionally regulated. A key question for us to ask ourselves is 'is this behaviour/response age appropriate' for the child? For example, in a pre-school setting you might not expect the child to have this level of understanding and be able to express it. In many cases, children do not know what they need, which is similar to when a baby cries. When this occurs, it is the adult's responsibility to interpret the feelings and communication, to process it and pass it back to the child in an understandable and safe manner. This sounds simple but is a finely nuanced process as it can be experienced as overly intense and perhaps even persecutory for the individual if they are not ready to receive the feelings fed back to them.

Reading this chapter you may have noticed the frequent reference to feelings. The links between experiences that influence our feelings, and that drive our behaviour, run throughout our work. Therefore, close attention is necessary, including consideration of our own feelings. When children present behaviours that challenge us, we will all have an emotional response that needs to be recognised and not confused with the feelings of the child/young person.

Practice Example 3

Isla is a fifteen-year-old girl placed in a secure setting. She is considered 'extremely bright' and, although not diagnosed, is thought to possibly have ADHD. She often gets cross in the classroom, particularly before break-time, screwing up her work, throwing it away and becoming agitated. When Steph, a teaching assistant, tries to offer support, Isla often shouts 'I hate you! You're the worst grown-up at this stupid place' before walking away. This occurs most days.

Situations like the above often leave staff feeling frustrated, worn-down, cross and confused. Most of our work settings are already strewn with stresses and anxieties, and taking the child's behaviour as a personal affront is not uncommon, especially when the child is verbally directing the behaviour at you, as Isla does each day. At these times it is helpful when our colleagues remind us that the behaviours are an expression of a child's feelings, which perhaps for Isla was a sense of anxiety that her work was not good enough. The practice example also highlights the difficulty in recognising the overlaps between neurodiversity, particularly when not diagnosed and that we know are much higher for children in the care system (Gajwani & Minnis, 2023), and children's trauma and the complexity this adds to making sense of their behaviour.

It is also important to recognise that the child/young person may be communicating more than one feeling at once; for example, Isla might be feeling anxious, but also excited about completing the work and going out to break.

Links between Behaviour and Communication

There exists a strong association between behaviour and children's ability to communicate (Lindsay & Dockrell, 2010). More than 80% of children recognised as having social, emotional and mental health difficulties (SEMH) have significant communication needs (Royal College of Speech and Language Therapists, 2024; NHS, 2018), while over two-thirds of children at risk of exclusion in schools have speech, language and communication needs (RCSLT, 2020). If we consider this association, perhaps it helps us understand what might be going on for a child. For example, is the child who refuses to follow the task set by the teacher being wilfully difficult? Perhaps, but maybe they are struggling with the model of communication and so are unclear of the task. So, why don't they put their hand up and ask for clarification? Well, that would assume the child is consciously aware of what is going on, which is unlikely. The child is more likely to be responding to the feelings that arise from not understanding the task and perhaps feeling 'I know you don't understand me and that makes me worried/scared'.

The feeling of being worried is not unusual for children. All children need to understand their feelings and how to use appropriate words to describe these. However, for a child with language difficulties, finding the right words is even harder. This means they will find emotion regulation more difficult and thus revert to unconscious and physiological responses such as fight, flight, freeze or fawn (Donahue, 2020). Knowing this places greater emphasis on us to provide opportunities to express and learn to understand feelings so they do not have to be exhibited through behaviours that challenge us.

Helping children develop non-verbal and verbal ways to express these feelings reduces the need for them to use behaviour as a primary form of communication. This includes teaching them how to express their feelings, how to ask for help, and how to resolve conflicts. It is often helpful for staff to model these communication skills through, for example, using feelings cards to point to at the start of each session/day or through morning check-ins. It is also important for staff to explore their own feelings, together, through developing an open, non-judgemental school culture. When children are alongside a member of staff who can self-regulate their own emotional state then the child learns to self-regulate. Such a culture can be developed through encouraging staff to share feelings in meetings through, for example, inviting colleagues to respond to questions such as: How are people feeling today? What feelings or emotions are people bringing to this meeting today?

Pause for thought: Imagine starting the day with energy, optimism and passion, but by the end feeling drained, deskilled and questioning what you have achieved. In your workplace do you get the opportunity to stop and think why your work makes you feel like that, and what do you do with those feelings?

Curiosity and Reflecting on the Meaning of Behaviour

Curiosity is one of the greatest tools we have in our box to try to make sense of behaviour. It is unlikely that the children will be able to articulately tell you what they are feeling and why they behave as they do. It is more likely that their behaviour is an unconscious expression of how they are feeling. So how do we make sense of someone else's unconscious behaviours? Curiosity is an excellent starting point. Being alongside a child and asking curiously: 'I can see you hiding behind the coats; I wonder whether you are feeling worried about break time?', for example, encourages us to wonder aloud about what might be happening with the child, rather than telling them why they are doing something. It allows staff to support children to make cognitive links between body and brain to support children to recognise their own behaviours.

Pause for thought: Can you think of a time when your responses to a child might have escalated their behaviour? Perhaps because you were feeling cross, overwhelmed or anxious?

As discussed in Chap. 2, reflection underpins much of the work offered by the Mulberry Bush. Such reflection encourages staff in a wide range of organisations, to make sense of these feelings with a central question being, 'whose feelings are you feeling'? Are these really your feelings, or are you a receptacle for the feelings of others, perhaps a child or young person you have been working alongside? There is also the possibility that it a bit of both. To recognise this requires self-reflection. When we consider behaviour as a communication, we tend to focus on the child/young person's behaviour. But how often do we step back to reflect on ourselves, our behaviour and reactions? How hard is it for us to admit that perhaps the child did not like what we did either?

Our ability to reflect on how we are feeling and the impact we have on situations and individuals is central to seeing behaviour as a communication, though the enormity and complexity of this should not be underestimated. We all see situations differently and have different perspectives, which are impacted by what we bring to the situation—remember the kaleidoscope idea. These differences can become exaggerated when we work in teams where often people have contrasting approaches and responses.

Pause for thought: Think about those you work closely with. Would a child/young person experience each of you differently? What personal experiences do you bring to your work and what cultural expectations and backgrounds? What enables each member of the team to have meaningful experiences with this child or young person?

When working in teams we often strive for consistency, but due to the different personalities and experiences of staff, teams frequently include a variety of contrasting approaches. In addition, staff will have different mood states depending on what is happening for them in their lives.. For example, a children's home for primary aged children once reported differences in how children were allowed to eat pizza—was it finger or knife and fork food? The children were quick to tell a new staff member they were wrong and 'didn't know anything', leaving the staff member feeling deskilled and disempowered. However, in a subsequent reflective team meeting, the team were able to explore that perhaps the children were feeling worried about how to eat the pizza in case the new person told them they were 'doing it wrong' or took it away from them. This understanding was only achieved through open discussion in team meetings that focused on how everyone was left feeling—something the new staff member found extremely strange and initially outside of their comfort zone.

Using team meetings in this way allowed staff to support one another by reflecting and thinking about the sadness, anger and at times, the hatred they were left feeling. Helping each other make sense of these powerful feelings allowed them to return each day, often to face new behaviours and feelings from the children. The topic of staff support will be discussed in greater depth in Chap. 7, Staff Support, and Chap. 8, Keeping Children at the Heart of Collaborative Working.

Six Stages of Distress

We often hear professionals say that 'the behaviour came from nowhere', but perhaps the question is 'were we looking at the right time and for the right things?'. Behaviour never comes from nowhere and the six stages of distress, based on Kapler and Wheelan's work around violence and the assault cycle (1980), can be a useful tool to help staff make sense of what is happening for a child/young person before, during and after a period of distress (Fig. 4.1).

Practice Example 4

Andrej was an eight-year-old child in a busy mainstream school. We were asked to support his staff team because they were concerned about his behaviours. With our support, staff completed a Six Stages of Distress grid, below, to try and step back and see what might be happening for Andrej before, during and after his periods of distress and to plan informed and proactive responses. Using this model, staff were able to share their collective experiences of Andrej and develop a plan that they could all work with.

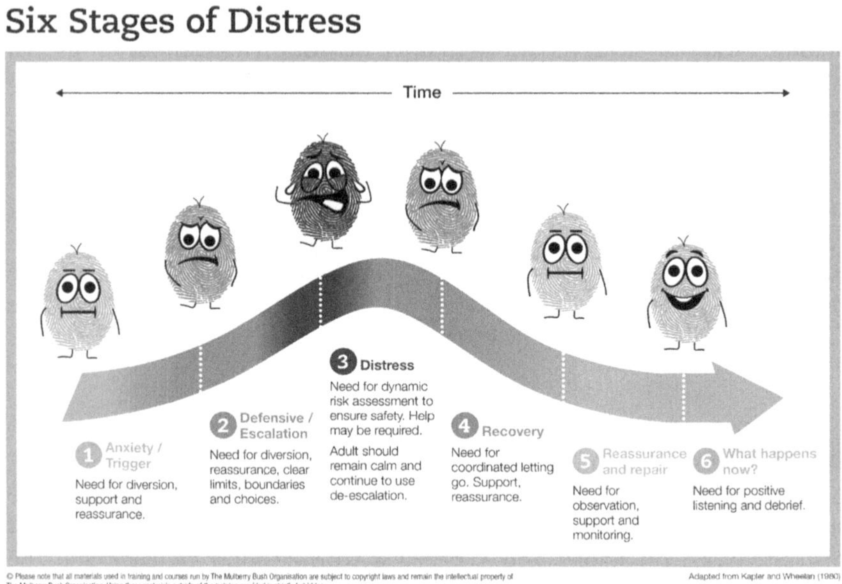

Fig. 4.1 Six stages of distress

Stage	*Presenting behaviour*	*Possible communication*	*Intervention*
1—Anxiety / trigger	*Withdraws from the group, uncooperative, wanders around the room*	*I am feeling worried, frustrated/upset*	*Be alongside Andrej early, offer reassurance. Diversion and distractions work well at this stage*
2—Defensive / escalation	*Raised voice, swearing, screwing up work, increased movement around the room*	*I am feeling anxious / starting to feel overwhelmed*	'I can hear you are talking with a louder voice. I wonder if you are feeling cross. Let's go and find some outdoor space' / *physical activity*

(*Continued*)

Stage	Presenting behaviour	Possible communication	Intervention
3—Distress	*Shouting, running, kicking and hurting*	*I need to move; I can feel tension in my body / I need to escape—I can't cope* *I feel anxious so I am making lots of noise to fill the space*	*Provide space away from others but allowing Andrej to know you are close by for support. Engage with him, kick a ball with him*
4—Recovery	*Reluctant to talk and unable to stay still, can return quickly to distressed behaviours*	*I am worried I'll be blamed / Will you still like me? I'm emotionally worn out*	*Reassurance / take plenty of time before rejoining the class / offer physical movement to re-connect*
5—Reassurance and repair	*Talks about feeling stupid and worthless, uses baby voice*	*Low self-esteem / I'm not good enough / I just want to be looked after*	*Continue to reassure verbally and offer something from his personalised box*
6—What happens next	*Go through the incident with Andrej—Verbally or through drawing. Talk about the feelings he might have been feeling*	*Andrej talks about what happened and reassurance that he is not 'thick' and that his behaviour can change, with support*	*Offer reassurance, not just now but over the next few days*

The six-stages of distress model recognises that the stages do not occur in a linear process because children do not always move smoothly between stages, and nor do all children sit in all stages. For many children, particularly those who have experienced early life trauma, like Andrej, they may constantly be in heightened states of stages two, three and four. However, stepping back from the behaviour and reflecting more holistically on the child helps us understand the communication behind the behaviour, and the unmet needs that might need meeting.

Consider the Five Rs

Models of seeing behaviour as communication are freely available but here, we share a model of the Five Rs (adapted from Education Scotland n.d.). This is not meant to be prescriptive but a helpful framework to add to your toolbox and bring together the issues discussed within this chapter. In other words, it is a way to step back from feeling the need to 'manage' the behaviour and move towards making sense of what is happening (Fig. 4.2).

Fig. 4.2 Five Rs

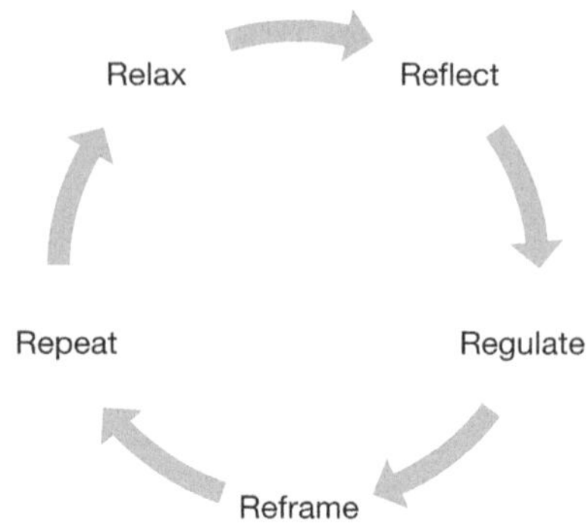

Practice Example 5

Leandra had been key working and supporting Samina, aged fifteen, at an independent children's home for four years. Samina had made good progress and almost completely stopped her physical aggression, her absconding and her refusal to join in with the other children. It was approaching the time when she was getting ready to leave and discussions were happening about a possible move to foster carers. Everyone felt this could be a positive step for Samina, but as the move got closer, she started to exhibit the behaviours she had shown when she first arrived, as well as rejecting care and support. Leandra was left feeling sad, overwhelmed and questioning whether she had let Samina down and if the decision to move Samina was right.

Reflect

Leandra's first step was not just to observe the behaviour but to carefully consider the context, the environment and possible unmet needs. Behaviours don't happen in isolation!

She asked herself:

- What was Samina doing and what might this be telling her? *Her earlier behaviours had required lots of close adult support; was she asking for this again?*
- What did she know about Samina's background? When her behaviours become challenging, her placements were brought to an abrupt

halt. Was she trying to achieve this as a means of avoiding a painful ending, perhaps?

- How was she left feeling? Scared, anxious? Whose feelings were these? *Leandra felt overwhelmed with feelings of loss but also pride. Maybe these matched Samina's feelings?*
- What support might she need? (see Chap. 7 for further discussion.) *Leandra's manager had been off sick and Leandra had missed her last two monthly supervisions, just when she needed them most.*

Regulate

Words such as 'regulate' are used more frequently now but often only with regard to the child/young person. Leandra found it helpful that she was asked:

- Why does Samina evoke such strong feelings in you? Is she looking to recreate familiar relationship patterns? *Leandra had experienced her own difficulties with her mother, who had rejected her when she was younger—she now experienced Samina's rejection of her making her realise that she and her mother had never talked about that period of her life.*
- What are your triggers? Which of your buttons will be pushed? *Leandra identified that Samina shouting 'your mum is dead' made her angry and she would, unconsciously, withdraw from Samina.*
- Are you working in isolation? Work with children's trauma needs to be done with others; remember Chap. 2's discussion about staff being trauma-focused. As a worker you should not feel on your own, even if the child/young person leaves you feeling you are in isolation. *Leandra worked as part of a small team but as keyworker felt alone with Samina, much as Samina felt alone.*

Reframe

I have lost count of how many times settings have spoken about a child whose behaviour is 'attention seeking'. Almost all the examples were helpfully reframed towards whether this might be relationship/'need' for attention from a child who struggles to articulate, or understand, much like Poppy in Chap. 2. People often describe the behaviour rather than the child, so this needs reframing. The child cannot change the narrative on their own; we must guide them. Remember, in Chap. 2 we discussed the need for relational work.

Samina was ignoring your instructions and requests	To	She may have become so alert to everything around them that she cannot hear the instructions
Samina refused any help Leandra offered	To	Samina may have needed clarity and was left feeling 'helpless' and out of control because decisions were being made about where/with whom she would live
Samina looked sulky and wouldn't speak	To	She may have had no words to describe how she felt, 'sulking' was, perhaps, her only means of communication
Samina was having another meltdown	To	Samina had lost the ability to regulate her feelings, or perhaps was still dysregulated

Repeat

Repetition reinforces understanding and helps create a sense of emotional safety on which to build the capacity to explore feelings and thoughts further. Leandra tried to:

- go back to earlier behaviours with Samina, even when this was difficult, and notice aloud that things have improved.
- repeat the reassurance that she could support Samina, particularly at times when she was not distressed, as this was when Samina could hear her most.
- Spend time with Samina when she was regulated, not just when she was dysregulated.

Relaxation

Working with behaviours that challenge can be physically and emotionally exhausting. How do you, and perhaps your setting, enable you to:

- Relax and have time for yourself—*Leandra had to make sure she didn't take on all the overtime shifts so she had time to continue her sports activities.*
- Maintain a sense of humour as this can help keep things in perspective and not take them personally.

- Be patient and realistic with yourself. Traumatised children with disrupted attachments often require time to change—the work does not happen overnight.

Conclusion

It is clear that the concept of seeing behaviour as a communication of an unmet need is complex. In times of difficulty and distress, it can require a paradigm shift of thinking from 'how do I stop this behaviour?' towards 'what may be happening for this child?'. It is not a one-off intervention, but part of the development of a culture of understanding and reflecting on behaviours. To be successful, it needs embedding across all parts of the organisation and at all levels. This can be challenging because not all organisations encourage this level of reflection or find it valuable. When introducing the concept of behaviour as a communication, we often start by working collaboratively with the leadership team to support the development of the culture through practice and, of course, through the policies that guide the settings. Chapter 8 explores the Mulberry Bush core concept of collaborative working and the difficulties that can arise when working in this manner across wider settings.

References

Den Heijer, A. (2018). *Nothing you don't already know: Remarkable reminders about meaning, purpose, and self-realization.* CreateSpace Independent Publishing Platform.

Donahue, J. J. (2020). Fight-flight-freeze system. In V. Zeigler-Hill & T. K. Shackelford (Eds.), *Encyclopedia of personality and individual differences.* Springer.

Education Scotland. (n.d.). *Regulate, relate, reason and restore.* Retrieved February 5, 2025, from https://education.gov.scot/media/4a3dm1un/regulate-relate-reason-restore-information-note-informed-level.pdf

Fonagy, P., & Target, M. (2003). Psychoanalytic theories. *Perspectives from developmental pathology.*

Gajwani, R., & Minnis, H. (2023). Double jeopardy: Implications of neurodevelopmental conditions and adverse childhood experiences for child health. *European Child & Adolescent Psychiatry, 32*(1), 1–4.

Jacobs, M. (2012). *The presenting past* (4th ed.). Open University Press.

Kapler, S. G., & Wheelan, E. G. (1983). Survival skills for working with potentially violent clients. *Social Casework, 64*(6), 339–346.

Lindsay, G., & Dockrell, J. (2010). *The relationship between speech, language and communication needs (SLCN) and behavioural, emotional and social difficulties (BESD)*. Department for Education.

NHS Digital. (2018). *Mental health of children and young people in England, 2017*, https://digital.nhs.uk/data-and-information/publications/statistical/mental-health-of-children-and-young-people-in-england/2017/2017

Price, H., Jones, D., Herd, J., & Sampson, A. (2018). Between love and behaviour management: The psychodynamic reflective milieu at the Hill view school. *Journal of Social Work Practice*, Routledge, *32*(4), 391–407.

Royal College of Speech and Language Therapists. (2020). *Speech and language therapists supporting pupils in alternative provision*. Retrieved March 23, 2025, from https://www.rcslt.org/wp-content/uploads/2024/05/RCSLT_ALT_Provision_2020.pdf

Royal College of Speech and Language Therapists. (2024). *Understanding the links between communication and behaviour*. Retrieved March 19, 2025, from https://www.rcslt.org/wp-content/uploads/media/Project/RCSLT/rcslt-behaviour-a4-factsheet.pdf

CHAPTER 5

What to Do About Strong Feelings?

Siobhan Foster-Weston and Caryn Onions

Introduction

This chapter explores the strong feelings which can be evoked in children, staff and their carers when offering help and support. It focuses on the interplay between physical safety, emotional safety, boundaries and therapeutic work. It also considers what happens when staff have different views and different tolerance levels.

Practice Example 1

We were supporting a staff team setting up a new therapeutic community for children who had experienced early life trauma and no longer lived with their families. Most of the staff were new to this work but only a few had worked reflectively. Most had not had the experience of thinking about the meaning behind children's unpredictable and chaotic behaviours. When we first met, I could see they were grappling with and trying to make sense of their very powerful feelings. Some were jealous of others, assuming they had an easier time, especially getting children to do what they were asking them to do. Others wanted to know how to manage the children's behaviour as they felt powerless and out of control. Feelings of despair were palpable, and people did not seem able

C. Onions et al., *Supporting Children and Young People with Complex Needs*, Palgrave Texts in Counselling and Psychotherapy,
https://doi.org/10.1007/978-3-032-16699-9_5

to support to each other, so the group felt a lonely and dysfunctional place.

Pause for thought: Have you ever felt powerless in your work and resented colleagues who you felt were having a better experience than you? In those moments how have you found resolution and what helped to make sense of the strong feelings that were evoked in you?

As in the practice example above, helplessness in the caring professions is a complicated yet commonly recognised feeling. We discussed this briefly in Chap. 2 and described it as a combination of the child 'leaving' their unwanted thoughts and feelings with the adult, alongside the adult's own reaction to the situation (Ironside, 2004). This has been and will be a common theme throughout the book, and we encourage you to look back at the previous three chapters. Nevertheless, it is an uncomfortable feeling to not know what to do to support a child or young person with their overwhelming feelings and then to grapple with the resentments between colleagues or family members that arise from this. The frustration when a child rejects help time and time again can lead us to wonder 'if only they would just let me help them' and 'why are they rejecting me when I only want to keep them safe?'. This will be a familiar experience to adults who work and live with children who have suffered trauma, and they will understand that this is a crucial part of the child's journey.

It is normal for individuals working in a team around a child to approach the work in slightly different ways. Our individual ability to tolerate challenging behaviour as well as our response to conflict will vary hugely. Due to our unique life experiences, we all react differently to obstacles, defiance and provocation. However, when the task of a team is to look after and provide children with consistent care and treatment, then these differences can be problematic, especially when they are not spoken about and remain unacknowledged.

Exploring the strong feelings within a team is never easy and will often generate tension. This is what happened when one of us worked with the group in practice example 1, supporting them to learn to work together. Working with a team at this foundational level means that staff can rely on each other when situations become more complex. Over time, the team was able to feel safe enough to acknowledge the strain and unease that could arise when working closely together in tense situations. They began to acknowledge and explore how different individuals within the group were left feeling by the children's behaviour towards them. As time went on, they discussed specific incidents where conflict had emerged; for example, when some staff had allowed the children sweets on a different day to what had been agreed. As the individuals in the group spoke to each other about what was happening within the child group and their individual interactions, it became clear that the children were testing boundaries and finding gaps between the staff members. This is normal childhood behaviour that occurs all the time in families but is more complicated when a team of adults are involved. The staff could clearly see how these inconsistencies left the children feeling confused and unsure. Because of our regular meetings, the group started to work more closely together. Sharing their differences gave them space to understand their different perspectives as well as finding some commonality, which, over time, helped to develop their own unique culture.

This practice example shows that the therapeutic work needs to begin with the adults, in this case, a team of residential workers. They needed to get to know each other and to understand their differences. This led to deeper conversations about practice and how they could support each other during the tricky times at work.

Therapeutic childcare is multi-layered, as it often involves numerous interpersonal relationships that crisscross in many directions. This chapter explores the multifaceted aspect of therapeutic relational work by using four practice examples. You have already read the first one, which focused on the importance of people who work in therapeutic teams. In that setting, the crucial part of therapeutic work is underpinned by all team members exploring their feelings about doing the work as a team. It deepens understanding about each child and allows colleagues to work out how best to support each other. It is the bedrock to providing physical and emotional stability that underlies therapeutic practice.

The second practice example looks at a similar issue for adopters in a family setting. Without a backup team, the physical and emotional environment will be unstable. We consider child-to-parent violence as a risk factor.

The third practice example is from a residential setting and explores the way in which safety and stability need to be in place before helping children start to talk and think about their experiences.

The final practice example is based in a nurture group in a mainstream primary school. It outlines how nurture principles can support children who struggle to settle and feel safe enough to learn.

Aims of the Chapter

This chapter

- explores how to provide a physical and emotional environment so that a child can feel safe
- discusses what happens next, once they start to feel safe enough to explore their trauma and their feelings;
- considers the impact of strong feelings on the adults working and living alongside them and
- examines how to validate the child's strong feelings by living with and tolerating their emotional pain, knowing they are not alone, and that we can survive the pain with them.

Practice Example 2

Lianna is nine. She loves to dance, climb trees and doesn't go anywhere without her teddy. She hates broccoli, loud noises and appears scared of people she doesn't know. For Lianna and her four siblings, her early years were confused, unpredictable and frightening. There would often be unfamiliar adults in the family home, and her mother was a known heroin user. Lianna is adopted and initially seems to settle in well to the family home. However, after a few months she displays chaotic and disruptive behaviour. Lianna often punches and kicks her adoptive mum, and the violence is getting worse as she is getting bigger. The family feel helpless. They feel like they are failing her and are not sure they can survive as a family much longer.

Pause for thought: How do adoptive families create their own support networks to help them survive painful and intense feelings?

When working with adoptive families we often hear about the heartache they face when their child starts to process their trauma through dysfunctional and often violent behaviour. The intensity of this behaviour in a family setting can feel unmanageable. Without a 'team' around them, it can be very isolating (Donovan, 2014). When professionals work with challenging behaviours it can also be difficult and intense, and it is not unusual for staff to question whether they can carry on with the work. Ideally, they would be able to access support structures, and through conversations with colleagues would gain important knowledge that recognising, understanding and then tolerating a child's high levels of distress is a vital part of the journey. This is explored in more detail in Chap. 7. They would also learn that it is likely to get better and, importantly, they are able to leave work at the end of the day and have a break from the intensity. These strategies that staff rely on to build resilience and the ability to survive are sadly not readily available to most families. Therefore, it is important that they are able to create these, while recognising that their support systems are likely to look different. We return to this at the end of the section.

Adoptive parents are parents: they are not professionals, and they are not able to walk away at the end of a long day. They are parents who love and care for their children, who are being emotionally and physically tested to see if they can survive their child's trauma-related behaviours. The child will need to see if their parents can keep them safe, if they are able to tolerate and survive their trauma with them, rather than behave in the unhelpful ways the child has previously experienced other adults. In a family setting it can feel much harder to say 'no' to a child when that parent knows they will be faced with the fallout of their decision, as no one else is going to pick up the pieces. The parents also need to hold many different roles for the child. For example, a common role is that of an advocate for the child who is struggling at school and whose distress will impact homelife. In these situations, parents will often have to fight get the supportive interventions their child needs.

We often encounter adoptive families who feel worn down by the lack of support available. A common theme is feeling like they are failing their children, and this easily escalates when the child rejects the parent who tries to help. It can be hard for adoptive parents to believe that things will get better, as they usually do not have the same breadth of experience and knowledge that residential staff have. They can feel deskilled at managing very challenging behaviours, often without a support network around them. This is supported by research that suggests that adopters' levels of commitment are 'associated with their feelings of "hope" about the future, feelings that [are] closely linked to the level, accessibility and quality of the therapeutic and professional resources available' (Bardsley, 2017, p. 120).

Adoptive families can also worry about how they will keep themselves and their child safe when the child displays very risky behaviours. Child to parent violence contributes to adoptive parents feeling helpless, inadequate and isolated (DfE, 2014). Although this is also a worry for staff in schools and residential settings, they will have robust risk management structures in place and a collective response to managing the uncertainty, including clear procedures to follow when a child is being unsafe. Unfortunately, in a family this is often a different scenario. Children who have experienced trauma can have less awareness of risk, putting themselves in situations that could have serious consequences. This leads parents to be on constant alert to the possibility of responding to violence, which can feel overwhelming and frightening (Golm, 2024).

To survive this challenging time and create a home that is physically and emotionally safe, families need to create their own support structures: to know who they can turn to when they need to walk away for a couple of hours; to allow them to walk back in feeling a little more resilient. The first steps of doing this can be challenging for the parents as it requires them to be honest about their feelings towards the situation. Acknowledging that they are struggling can feel like they are failing. Parents need support from professionals to enable them to reframe this so they can feel like they are the experts when it comes to looking after their child. To repeatedly do this to the best of their ability needs solid support.

Sometimes this support network can be family and friends, and sometimes it will need to include others such as other adoptive families who understand their situation, respite care and holiday clubs that can understand their child's needs. Support groups where other people share their experiences can be reassuring and validating, and families do say how invaluable they can be (Awoyemi et al., 2025). Any parent in isolation needs the support of others to create a safe environment for their child. Without this, parenting children on the edge of school and family life will be precarious.

Practice Example 3

Amari is referred to the Mulberry Bush. She has been at the school for a few weeks, and the initial settled calm period is over. In the past week, Bill, her experienced keyworker, has noticed that she is getting into arguments with other children: she snatches their toys, hits them and is unsafe. Amari does not yet trust Bill to let him help her at these times, so it often happens that they get into an argument too. Bill is familiar with this situation and understands that with time Amari will start to invest in the school and allow staff to help her.

Pause for thought: How do you help children to feel safe within their environment to allow their journey of recovery to begin? When is it okay to say to them that you see their difficulties?

How Do We Facilitate a Child's Journey Through Their Placement?

During our careers at the Mulberry Bush, we have become more aware of the enormity of what we ask of the children during their placement. Even when they first begin, they are expected to make relationships with adults and children they have never met before, and to follow rules that may make no sense to them. During their time with us we want them to tell us what has happened in their short lives and find ways to leave behind the defences they have built up (to protect them from the pain of their trauma) so we can help them make sense of why they are at the Mulberry Bush to start their journey of recovery. This therapeutic work is a huge task for the child and needs to be done safely, thoughtfully and carefully, and at their pace.

Carers experienced in working with children who have suffered early complex trauma will understand that the child's journey is likely to be long, painful and complicated, but if supported in a thoughtful and compassionate way the impact can be positive and long-lasting. I often think of a child's journey at the Mulberry Bush as the starting point of a lifetime of recovery and sensemaking. Hopefully the children will integrate the building blocks on which to grow and keep grounded and can access them when the next hurdle arrives.

Before we start to unravel the child's trauma, they must feel safe within their physical environment. We are not simply referring to the buildings and grounds but to the culture and the emotional containment (Onions & Browner, 2012). This involves the child's strong emotions being taken in and managed by the adult (Bion, 1962). To achieve this there need to be boundaries that are clear and predictable: the child needs to know what is happening, what is expected of them, and why these expectations are being asked of them. Like Amari in practice example 3, most of the children that we care for will not have experienced a consistent, reliable carer in their lives. This leads them to be suspicious of staff, and they often respond in fight, flight, freeze or fawn as they are unable to predict how caregivers will respond to them (Howe, 2005).

A therapeutic response to this situation could entail creating a small and predictable world so the child feels safer and can slowly expand their emotional world to include more experiences, develop more relationships, and feel more secure. It mirrors how babies are helped to explore and experience the world from the safety of their parents' arms. It may sound simple but providing children with these frameworks will not be straightforward. They are likely to resist the structures and push to see how far they can test the adults' boundaries to see if they remain consistent. Once a child begins to trust adults then, over time, they will be able to let themselves be looked after. If the adults can survive this period, then they too will feel confident that they can offer the children emotional containment.

Negotiation and Boundaries

Affronti et al. (2015) interviewed eighteen young people in early adulthood who had grown up in in foster care. In terms of consistency and rules, they wrote.

> Participants noted that rules helped them [...] to form healthy habits, especially if ground rules were established early and adhered to over time. Retrospectively, they indicated that consistent rules also created a sense of 'home,' helped instil respect, and encouraged them to be responsibly productive. (Affronti et al., 2015, p. 10)

It is vital that carers think openly, creatively, collaboratively and flexibly around the boundaries and structures that are in place. Constant review is needed to make sure that there is a consistent and predictable approach, which is both meeting the needs of the individual child and the group. Changing a routine every week is unlikely to be helpful for the child as it will feel chaotic. However, enforcing a rule just because it has always been done that way is also not in the child's best interest. Wondering and being curious about what we do and why we do it is best practice. As mentioned previously, it is also important that carers are on board with what is agreed. The child's voice also needs to be heard. Interestingly, in recent years it feels as though as a society we have become more mindful of the importance of this.

The child needs to feel as if there can be some negotiation and that they are being given some authority in decisions that involve them. Having these discussions can slowly increase their understanding of relationships and how people can manage to live together. When the child has too much control, they can feel scared, which can lead them to be reckless. We are always balancing these factors: we may not always get it right, but we need to reflect on our practice to tease out the parts that have been successful and the parts that can be improved. Returning to a child after an incident has happened, to help them explore what has taken place, is crucial for learning—and is a legal requirement in education settings—but often the child will have a different view of events that have happened (DfE, 2015). There may have been key factors that triggered the behaviour that could be avoided in the future. Therefore, if we are able to hear what the child feels, we can develop our practice accordingly.

This is the beginnings of the therapeutic work. The child begins to feel safe as the world around them becomes more predictable and they reliably see adults as people who can look after them. Being listened to and helped to find their voice builds a positive self-image and self-worth. It is through these repeated experiences that traumatised children genuinely start to understand who they are and tease out what they think and feel. This is an important turning point. The importance for children of experiencing carers who show up, day after day, even when things are tough, cannot be underestimated. It is invaluable for the child that the adult will and can survive the difficult times and help them in a non-retaliatory way make sense of their confused behaviour and distressing thoughts and feelings.

Exploring Painful Feelings

When the child is feeling safer and more secure in their relationships and environment, this is when they may be able to begin to explore the trauma they have experienced. As previously mentioned, this journey will look different for all children, and it is crucial that carers are emotionally in tune with the individual's capacity and capabilities. Not pushing them too soon in the exploration and thinking creatively how this process will differ for each child is an important element. At the Mulberry Bush, each child's treatment team will contribute to the thinking about how to adapt the approach and who is best to undertake this next step of the work.

The child needs to feel that they will not be judged or shamed for their experiences (Price et al., 2018). Adults need to remain sensitive to the fact that despite the child suffering mistreatment from others, these others are also significant people in their lives, and the child is likely to have complicated feelings towards them that need to be respected and acknowledged by staff. Allowing the child the time and space to explore these feelings is important, alongside developing less destructive ways of processing the feelings, so they are more manageable. Nevertheless, the reality is that for most children the process of recovery from their trauma will need to happen over many years. If the process continues in the right direction there will not be an end point but a gradual reworking of early relationships. It is akin to mourning the loss of a stable, carefree childhood. It is not unusual for children to go through periods of feeling more or less settled, especially around the time of certain anniversaries or a significant event. This is likely to put them back in touch with their trauma, which can lead to an upsurge in feelings that can be overwhelming and scary for the child. It can be a slow process, but the important thing is that they are not alone.

Practice Example 4

Oscar started his local primary school in reception and was quickly singled out as the badly behaved, naughty child who would not sit still nor follow the teaching staff's requests. Other children seemed fearful of him; they avoided him and would not include them in their play. Teaching staff were frustrated about the impact he had on the rest of the class and struggled to feel they were doing a good enough job for Oscar and the other children. Oscar did not understand why nobody liked him or wanted to be near him. He really wanted to have friends but did not know how to play and take turns. Oscar felt like the bad child that nobody liked or had time for—just like how he felt at home. Things at home seemed stable and his parents were puzzled as his older sister was enjoying school. Oscar joined a nurture group, where he began to settle and started to trust the staff, particularly Jill, who he liked to spend time with.

Pause for thought: Have you worked with or do you know a child like Oscar? How must it feel for children like Oscar who feel lost and overwhelmed in mainstream schools?

In this last section we continue with Oscar and review how the learning experience of some children in a mainstream classroom can be overwhelming rather than an environment where they can thrive. We will consider how the child's needs can be met and what positive outcomes for the child might look like.

Oscar's experience of school so far, is of being told he is naughty, having no one to play with, and feeling lonely and not good enough. These labels placed on children so young can have long-lasting effects. When a child's self-esteem and self-worth is affected like this it can take many years of focused support to not only shift other people's views of them but for them to also shift their own narrative.

A child like Oscar can be a puzzle to family and professionals as his home life seemed to be stable, although understandably his parents were pleased to get help and felt validated that staff were also concerned about him. Staff said he seemed aware that he was different to the other children, especially when other negative behaviours emerged. He could be disruptive or withdrawn and could struggle with basic interactions like turn taking or sharing. At such times other children would notice these differences and would react to them. If these interactions are not managed carefully by the teaching staff, then the negative feelings can intensify and children like Oscar will be quickly labelled as the naughty or the disruptive child. Often this is done without much thought, and the impact of these labels are not fully realised until much later in life.

Nurture is a relational approach to education that centres on identifying and meeting children's social and emotional developmental needs. It develops pupils' social skills, confidence, resilience and self-esteem (Nurture UK, 2025). Educationists Holmes and Boyd (1999) developed the following Six Principles of Nurture:

1. Children's learning is understood developmentally.
2. The classroom/school offers a safe base.
3. Nurture is important for the development of well-being.
4. Language is understood as a vital means of communication.
5. All behaviour is communication.
6. Transitions are significant in the lives of children.

When Oscar starts in the nurture group he is met with adults who accept his feelings. They understand that sitting still for long periods of time is difficult for him and they offer him many opportunities throughout the day for movement as they can see this is helpful. The staff demonstrate unconditional positive regard for him and see his behaviours as a way for him to communicate how he is feeling. They can tell when he is feeling tired because he has not had much sleep the night before and can adjust their plans to meet his needs. He is always offered breakfast in case he has not eaten.

Over time, Oscar starts to feel loved and cared for by Jill and the other adults in the group. They feel in touch with how he is feeling while helping him achieve and meet his goals. As the teaching staff get to know Oscar, they provide him with strategies that help him navigate the difficult parts of his day. His days are predictable but fun, and he is encouraged to find the joy in the smallest of things, such as flying a kite, playing conkers, or going on a treasure hunt. While the learning is important, feeling safe needs to happen to allow the learning to flourish.

When it is time for Oscar to leave the nurture group, he feels sad to say goodbye to Jill and the others who have helped him grow so much but he also feels more able to face the challenges of a bigger classroom. They have helped him recognise when things feel too much and he is starting to remember to ask for support. At some point Oscar may need to return to a smaller group, but for now he feels ready to face the next steps.

Early interventions in spaces like nurture groups are essential to help create safe environments for children to explore and be curious about learning. There need to be opportunities for staff to understand the individual needs of children and to adapt their provision, rather than expecting the child to conform to pre-existing school rules.

Take-Away Tips on Therapeutic Relational Practice

It could be argued that many of the elements of therapeutic practice that we have described in this chapter are routine, nothing out of the ordinary, ways of relating to children. The children's needs are central to the work, but above that the approaches are not new or complicated ways of working. You do not need to attend an expensive course; neither is there a sophisticated manual. That said, it is not easy work, and the way is unlikely to be straightforward. It might be difficult to sustain, but if you get it right it will bring huge satisfaction to you and the child. The Therapeutic Childcare Standards (Ury et al., 2025) were co-developed with the Mulberry Bush and might be useful. Here is a summary of the main points:

Working Therapeutically Means

- You may feel that you have made progress, only for it to be taken away.
- You may start to form relationships and then be rejected.
- Different children will evoke different feelings in different people. Staying with the uncomfortable feelings, the pain and the fear, is helpful.
- Children will provoke you to see how far they can go and whether you can tolerate and survive the worst of them.
- Whatever you do you may feel like it is not enough.

Watch out for these Team Dynamics (which Are Common and to Be Expected)

- Feeling jealous or frustrated with colleagues.
- Wondering if they are the better or preferred 'parent'.
- It is not only the children's behaviour that communicates 'hidden meanings'; this happens in teams too (see Chap. 4).

How to Survive the Work

- Go at the child's pace.
- Accept that there will be progress and regression.
- Recognise that it takes time—much longer than you anticipate.
- Stick with it, show up day after day and be authentic.
- Get support, supervision and a reliable group of colleagues to talk to.
- Make time to look after yourself and take good breaks.

Conclusion

Therapeutic relationship-based work has been the focus of this chapter. We began by describing the importance of creating an environment that is physically and emotionally safe. This is the fundamental principle of therapeutic work: without this, children will not feel safe enough to explore their thoughts, feelings and behaviour. Once they have established a trusting relationship with someone, they are more likely to tolerate being gently challenged and to start to have discussions about the reasons they are in foster care, adopted, in a residential setting or a special school. The staff or carers are their vehicle for change; therefore, effective staff support is crucial for the work to be sustainable.

References

Affronti, M., Rittner, B., & Semanchin Jones, A. M. (2015). Functional adaptation to foster care: Foster care alumni speak out. *Journal of Public Child Welfare, 9*(1), 1–21.

Awoyemi, B., May, L., David, R., Majumder, P., & Sayal, K. (2025). Quantitative and qualitative outcomes of non-violent resistance interventions for children and adolescents with emotional and behavioural difficulties and their caregivers—A systematic review. *Adoption & Fostering, 49*(2), 204–226.

Bardsley, K. (2017). Adopting children with high therapeutic needs: Staying committed over the long haul. *Adoption & Fostering, 41*(2), 120–130.

Bion, W. (1962). *Learning from experience*. Karnac.

Department for Education (DfE). (2014). *Beyond the adoption order: Challenges, interventions and adoption disruption*. Retrieved July 28, 2025, from https://www.gov.uk/government/publications/beyond-the-adoption-order-challenges-intervention-disruption

Department for Education (DfE). (2015). *Guide to the Children's Homes Regulations including the quality standards*. Retrieved July 28, 2025, from https://www.gov.uk/government/publications/childrens-homes-regulations-including-quality-standards-guide

Donovan, S. (2014). *The unofficial guide to adoptive parenting: The small stuff, the big stuff and the stuff in between*. Jessica Kingsley Publishers.

Golm, D. (2024). Breaking the taboo: Let's talk about child-to-parent violence. *Adoption & Fostering, 48*(2), 163–166.

Holmes, E., & Boyd, E. (1999). *The six principles of nurture*. Retrieved July 28, 2025, from https://www.nurtureuk.org/the-six-principles-of-nurture/

Howe, D. (2005). *Child abuse and neglect: Attachment, development and intervention*. Palgrave.

Ironside, L. (2004). Living a provisional existence: Thinking about foster carers and the emotional containment of children placed in their care. *Adoption & Fostering, 28*(4), 39–49.

Nurture UK. (2025). *Inclusive schools, empowered learners: The evidence for nurture practice*. Retrieved July 28, 2025, from https://www.nurtureuk.org/reports/evidence-for-nurture-2025/

Onions, C., & Browner, J. (2012). Spaces for growth: Where milieu therapy and psychotherapy meet. In A. Horne & M. Lanyado (Eds.), *Winnicott's children*. Routledge.

Price, H., Jones, D., Herd, J., & Sampson, A. (2018). Between love and behaviour management: The psychodynamic reflective milieu at the mulberry bush school. *Journal of Social Work Practice, 32*(4), 391–407.

Ury, L., Carver, K., Roberts, N., Dicken, S., Stanesby, C., & Thibaut B. (Eds.). (2025). *Therapeutic child care standards* (2nd ed.). Royal College of Psychiatrists. Retrieved August 22, 2025, from https://irct.org.uk/wp-content/uploads/2025/06/Childcare-standards.pdf?mc_cid=efbaf0737b&mc_eid=1a4104e65c

CHAPTER 6

Working Things Out with Children and Families

Caryn Onions

Introduction

This chapter explores working with families. It focuses on how we use therapeutic relationships to gain trust so we can deepen insight for families who feel stuck. Much of the work involves understanding loss and the impact on people's individual and family lives. By listening to and fully taking in the feelings that each person brings to the work, the practitioner can then start to tease out what is going on and why they might be trapped in painful or unhelpful repetitive ways of being together.

Practice Example 1

I remember, when I was a newly qualified social worker, meeting an adolescent girl and her single parent mother. The girl was refusing to go to school and her mother was desperate for help, as her employer would not pay her 'parent leave' for staying at home with her daughter. The mother said something like this:

I've no idea what she's thinking, and I always seem to get it wrong. I've been to a parenting group, I've tried so many things, but it just never works out, or if it does it doesn't last. I'm stressed out with worry but

C. Onions et al., *Supporting Children and Young People with Complex Needs*, Palgrave Texts in Counselling and Psychotherapy,
https://doi.org/10.1007/978-3-032-16699-9_6

at the same time I want to scream and make her talk. I end up feeling useless. I don't know what to do and the vicious circle starts again.

Pause for thought: Does this sound familiar to you? Have you spoken to a parent, foster carer or professional who describes their relationship with a child like this? If so, what did you do?

The meeting had only just started and before I had gleaned much information from either of them, they started to argue about the reason for coming to see me. I remember a rising sense of panic as they snapped and snarled at each other; I felt my heart beat faster and an overwhelming sense of wanting to tell them to shut up. At the same time, I remembered being an adolescent, and the triumphant thrill of arguing and being rude to my own mother. Meanwhile, my 'professional' internal voice was screaming at me to 'say something'. I now know that this jumble of thoughts and feelings belong to the concepts called 'transference' and 'countertransference'. When I trained as a social worker we were encouraged to be 'neutral' and not take into consideration our own responses to the work, whereas nowadays we value the use of the self in therapeutic work outside of the therapy room. This is illustrated by the following excerpt:

> The self I am interested in here is more a process than a 'thing'. It concerns our ability to scan, monitor, reflect upon, make sense of, and put to work our awareness of occupying a total field of experience (Ogden, 1999) in what I hope to have conveyed is a sophisticated and above all thoughtful and reflective manner. This 'field' is not just subjective, but inter-subjective, which means that we are attending to the continual impact of ourselves on others, and them upon us (Cooper, 2018)

With hindsight and experience, I could have used my rising sense of panic, irritation and identification with the adolescent to try to contain both of their worries and start to make emotional contact with their feelings and despair. This would have been an example of me occupying a state of mind able to hold the 'mess' that this mother and daughter were bringing to me. As a newly qualified social worker, this was unavailable to me, as I suspect it is to many new practitioners in a variety of settings. I was not experienced in psychodynamic practice at that stage of my career;

nor did I understand the impact that group and individual supervision and training could offer.

This chapter is about working with children and families, where family is taken in its widest context: it could be the child and their birth, foster or adoptive family, or with residential staff in loco parentis.

Aims of the Chapter

Four practice examples illustrate the complexity of children and young people with complex needs. While there are no solutions as such, they give an idea of how you might think differently about children and parents in your setting and how you might

- Consider some contemporary research examples of working with families with complex needs
- Demonstrate how professionals can use supervision and reflection to gather deeper understanding of familial relationships and
- Explore how to think differently about conversations between children and families to start to change the way they relate to one another.

What Does Contemporary Research Tell us about Working with Children and Families?

In this next section I report on three studies that examine what helps and hinders working with families with complex needs.

It is not unusual for the parents of children on the edge of school and family life to themselves be struggling with mental health needs. We know that children's difficulties rarely occur in isolation, and this research uncovered how unknowingly professionals concerned about a child may 'trigger a downward spiral of stressful processes', leaving parents feeling they lack control (Bacon et al., 2023, p. 1). Rather than improving things, this study suggests that parents can end up feeling marginalised and criticised instead of supported. Bacon et al. (2023) reported that parents with mental health needs can feel that the system is working against them, that the support offered is not what they want or need, and that services are constrained by being too rigid. Parents often have financial worries that tend to be excluded. Practitioners often intervene during a crisis, which means that their help is limited, fragmented and fails to take account of the whole picture (Bacon et al., 2023).

However, Redgate et al. (2024) researched edge-of-care interventions and found several key areas that consistently made a difference. First, they established that reflective and systematic parent and family skills training helped to promote family confidence in managing future situations. The most helpful trainings were when pro-social behaviours were promoted, helping to maintain the family unit. Second, a core mechanism for change is that these trainings should be home-based so that the worker can observe how and when difficulties arise and engage families in finding their own solutions. Third, a crucial aspect was the quality of the worker–family relationship, where trust, respect, and time enabled families to genuinely feel they were making the changes they needed rather than some approaches that left families feeling 'done-to or fixed' by the worker. This intensive work needs time, with a dedicated practitioner able to respond promptly to periods of high stress and emotional need. This would have an impact on worker caseloads.

The third study deals with the impact of family group conferences (FGC) on the prevention of children going into care. Originally from New Zealand, FGCs are meetings supported by an independent coordinator but led by family members. Their purpose is to plan and make decisions for children at risk, with the aim of agreeing how to keep them safe. The children's charity Coram undertook a randomised controlled study (RCT) and found that this approach significantly decreased the number of children in care one year after an FGC referral, that the likelihood of having care proceedings issued also decreased, and that children spent fewer days in care in the immediate six months following the FGC. While most families who took part did not feel as though the FGC made a major difference, most local authorities had a different view and thought they had played an important role (Taylor et al., 2023).

So what does this research tell us? The common features of these three studies are the importance of families and professionals working together, and for practitioners to really hear the voice of families. They do not specifically mention relational thinking, but that also seems at the core of these studies (Boden-Stuart & Larkin, 2024). They also capture the collaborative approach of the Mulberry Bush way of working. In the rest of the chapter, practice examples are used to explore the complexity of the work needed to support parents and children.

Using Reflection in Supervision

Practice Example 2

Logan, twelve, had been living with his 'youthful' yet exhausted grandparents, Jenni and Phil, for a while, as his single mother, Sinead, was in prison for drug-related crimes. While it was her first prison sentence, Sinead had been involved with the police for different offences for most of Logan's life. Once, when visiting Sinead in prison, Jenni saw an advert for a charity that helps families when a parent is in prison. Jenni contacted the charity, and Sian, family support worker, was allocated to the family. At the first home visit, Sian quickly learnt that Jenni and Phil were overwhelmed with everything that had happened. They had looked after Logan on and off for many years, but the arrangement had usually been for a week or so and usually prompted by Sinead needing a 'breather' and struggling to cope. They felt ashamed that Sinead was in prison and concerned about being judged as bad parents to Sinead. However, at the same time, they were afraid that Logan might be taken into care as things at home were nearing breaking point. They explained to Sian that Logan would often swear and threaten to hit them, and that he had started spitting at them. Also unbeknownst to Phil, Logan had started to 'clip Jenni around the ear'. She had kept it a secret but in one of these episodes her hearing aid was broken, and the story came out. Apparently, this had been going on for a while as Logan was doing this to Sinead before she went into prison. Sian experienced pressure from Phil to come up with the answer by saying things like 'We're counting on you to know what to do as we've tried everything', but when Sian explored what they had done it was difficult to offer any clear advice.

Sian brought the case to group supervision, telling colleagues she was unsure how to take things forward as Jenni was too scared to say anything to Logan, and Phil found discussing problems difficult. Colleagues asked her questions, made observations and explored how she was feeling about the work. Sian started to feel irritated and said she just wanted someone to tell her what to do, as she had lots of other cases to discuss. A colleague then wondered whether this mirrored what Jenni and Phil wanted: someone to tell them what to do, take away the painful, difficult feelings and smooth things over. The conversation then explored what might happen if Sian encouraged Jenni and Phil to lean into their feelings towards Logan—the violence and anger—to see whether they could come up with a plan together; something they all felt happy with, rather than something forced on them by Sian. The group also recognised that Jenni had kept this secret from Phil, and that Phil did not engage easily in conversations like these.

Pause for thought: Have you had times when you have been tempted to rush to offer advice, solutions and suggestions? Consider why you might have done that and how else you could have reacted.

In this group supervision, colleagues helped Sian see a possible connection between the feelings in the family and her countertransference response. Sian unconsciously was feeling like (identifying with) Phil: she wanted someone to give her an answer and tell her what to do, but, as we know, family dilemmas like this will have taken a long time to develop and are beyond simple behavioural advice. Jenni and Phil described layers of shame, and a psychodynamic way of thinking would suggest that Phil's need for a solution may have been unconsciously transformed into Sian's need, through processes of projection and identification. This is an unconscious mechanism where it is almost as if one person's feelings are expressed by someone else. It is also an example of how having trust in colleagues and reflecting on and sharing one's feelings about the work, can help deepen the understanding that ultimately helps children and families find a way through. We know that Phil found it difficult to talk about emotional topics, which is possibly why Jenni kept the violence a secret. Sian continued to meet Jenni and Phil, and after a few weeks Logan joined the conversation. This suggests that Jenni and Phil valued Sian's input, and that they trusted her enough to start a conversation with Logan.

Working with Parents in Groups

This next section is about a group of adopters who met regularly to think about the experience of adopting a child who is now struggling with family and school life. The practice example explores the repeated themes of the groups rather than any one child and family, as overall they shared common experiences. The group consisted of five adoptive couples: one couple were British Asian and the remainder were white British. One couple was in a same-sex relationship, while the remaining four were heterosexual couples. All their adopted children had high numbers of adverse childhood experiences (ACEs) in their early years, which affected significant areas of development, particularly their thinking, relating and behaviour. Most of the children also had at least one or more diagnoses such as attention deficit disorder, conduct disorder, attachment disorder, and autism.

Practice Example 3

Two of the couples in the group had a primary-aged child who was in a residential school as their special educational needs were not supported in mainstream education. The parents felt relieved but guilty that their child was not with them full-time at home, as things had become so difficult. The complexity of their feelings was palpable as they had all been desperate to become parents. Their children had experienced early-years neglect, and the resulting trauma was hard to bear, especially as they had waited so long for a family. Both couples revisited the fact that they were not told about the early history of their adopted children, but then in the same breath acknowledged that it would have been impossible for social workers to have known what had happened during the early months, when the birth mothers of their adopted children were so unwell physically and emotionally.

All the parents talked with disbelief that social care staff repeatedly failed to understand the difficulties at home and continued to question their parenting. They all felt negatively judged, and a common theme was that they were promised help and support before the adoption that failed to materialise. The same-sex couple felt they had been unfairly scrutinised during the adoption process. One couple thought they were being used like unpaid foster carers and that social care took advantage of people like them who wanted children. They all said they had to explain and justify to their own families why things were currently so difficult and repeatedly received unhelpful advice about behaviour management. On top of that, the Asian couple felt they were grappling with strong cultural beliefs from their heritage that clashed with their experience of growing up in the UK.

Two couples were struggling with their child's narrative around their birth story and why they did not live with their 'tummy mummies' anymore. One mother described 'life story work' as 'life saving work'. She found the impact on her child amazing but was worried that the person doing the work would not be able to continue for much longer.

The group facilitators worked hard not to take sides and to provide a balanced reflective perspective on everyone's experience, although one of them would get irritated when the group revisited the same topics. Containing the feelings of ten adults is hard work, and the facilitators welcomed time to talk together in supervision. They were worried about one couple whose relationship seemed precarious and another who could not see their child as anything other than violent, aggressive and determined to hate them.

Pause for thought: In your setting would a parent group be suitable? Are there parents grappling with similar issues who might benefit from a group?

This glimpse into an adopters' group highlights what a supportive yet difficult task it is for everyone. Emotions could run high, and the facilitators had to contain strong emotions. Feelings about the adopters' difficulties with their child were often mixed with the loss and grief of the couples whose reproductive journeys had been unsuccessful. The group members gradually came to trust the facilitators and each other and could speak openly about their feelings, safe in the knowledge that they would not be shamed, ridiculed or reported to social and healthcare.

The idea of collaborative and reflective working was also visible in the way the two facilitators worked together in the group, despite them also experiencing sometimes opposing views about the underlying reasons and feelings shared by the adopters. In supervision they wondered whether pairs of adopters had mixed views about their children and that was why the facilitators could sometimes have strikingly different thoughts and feelings despite them facilitating the same group. Reflection and collaboration enabled the full range of emotions to be expressed.

Repeated experiences like this will help parents mentalise and develop a better understanding of their own feelings as well as those of their child (Midgley et al., 2018). The support for each other helped enable adopters to make sense of their unique situations and, where necessary, make changes in their parenting (Di Lorenzo et al., 2023). Unravelling the parents' own difficulties and helping them see how changes they made might facilitate changes in their child was a constant element of the group's therapeutic aim. Helping the transition to parenthood is a major task for all parents, but especially important for adoptive couples as their relationships can become vulnerable when overwhelmed by looking after a child with such complex needs (Selwyn et al., 2015). Children were not included in the group, and in fact the group would not have been run along these lines had the children been present. It is an example of when it is not necessary to have the child take part in the work although they are omnipresent in all the discussions (Hill, 2025).

The next practice example looks at work with a mother and daughter.

Working with a Parent and Child Together

Practice Example 4

Emily and her mum had asked for help with Emily's school refusal. Emily was twelve, and her attendance at Greenfields secondary was dropping every term. She had loved junior school in her local village, where she knew all the staff and dinner ladies. She sometimes found the work a bit difficult, but her teacher always had time to go through it with her. Since her dad had taken his own life when she was eleven, she had started to feel scared not having him around anymore. Since moving up to Greenfields, her mum said she had 'lost her oomph' and didn't want to go out much anymore. Teachers wondered whether she had attention deficit disorder as she struggled to concentrate. Once a group of girls said something about her dad, which led her to avoid getting on the same bus. At first, she would attempt to walk to school to avoid the girls, but on other days she would hang around the shops. She eventually stopped leaving the house and only got to school if her mum drove her. The year head asked the school counsellor, Angie, to meet with Emily and her mum.

Angie met with them for about a term, and it quickly became clear that, since Emily's dad died, they both felt the need to hide away from the world and that the shock of his death was still reverberating powerfully. Emily's mum had been worried about her husband for a long time; Emily sensed that something was wrong and believed that she should have made things better. They were both silently blaming themselves for his death but had not been able to voice it until they spoke with Angie, not wanting to upset the other. A helpful conversation started when Emily said she was really worried about her mum dying: if she stayed home from school, she could keep an eye on her. Angie's involvement led them to start grieving together, plus she referred them to a local bereavement charity that organised events with other children and families.

In supervision, Angie talked about her impression that Emily and her mum were like two trains on parallel tracks going towards the same destination but never joining up. She often felt anxious with them, as if talking about feelings was like walking on eggshells. Bringing up the subject of Emily's dad was generally left to her, which felt exhausting.

Pause for thought: Have you had experience of helping children come back to school after divorce, loss or death of a parent?

This practice example describes a mother and daughter where feelings have got stuck and are having a detrimental impact on Emily's ability to access education. It is a good example of how people's thoughts and feelings can easily be misinterpreted, as the primary underlying issue was their difficulty in talking about how Emily's dad had died, whereas school staff were more focused on 'bullying', which turned out not to be the primary cause. Suicide and death are painful topics that Emily and her mum found difficult to talk about, and there was an underlying assumption that any discussion would be too painful and upsetting, perhaps reigniting the shock. We speculated that communicating about strong feelings was not part of their relationship, partly out of a need to protect each other, and they are likely to have minimised and pushed them away. It is a good example of how taking a trauma-informed approach, and looking under the surface at what was going on for each of them, enabled Emily to say she was worried about her mum dying—something her mum may not have considered. Angie also helped them find a new way of communicating, and perhaps this enabled them to go to the bereavement charity. Regular supervision helped Angie find ways to make links to Emily's dad's suicide in a trauma-informed and timely manner.

What Do these Practice Examples Say?

These four practice examples (adolescent and mother, Logan and grandparents, adopters' group and Emily and her mother), although different in their narrative detail, all involve the common elements of opening or improving communication between parents and children, and the use of staff supervision. To summarise:

First, in practice example 1, early in my career, I was not able to offer much containment to the mother and daughter, whereas in practice example 4 the school counsellor managed to open up the communication between the parent and child. The capacity to tolerate the emotional difficulties of others is in part the psychological ability of the practitioner but also depends on the ethos of the organisation, especially the support of employees.

Second, the importance of supervision cannot be underestimated, especially when helping children and young people struggling to engage in school and family life. Supervision is routinely accepted in the world of social work, therapy and counselling, but is rarely embedded in educational policy and teacher practice. However, 'teachers are faced with an increasingly complex environment in which they need significant support to foster the classroom climates their students benefit from' (Gardner et al., 2022, p. 370). The use of staff supervision in various settings is elaborated in Chap. 7.

Third, using groups to support parents can be an effective way in reducing seclusion and helping to create social networks for parents and families who have become isolated. They offer a safe place to share dilemmas, particularly when adults have social and mental health concerns about a child or young person. Despite what is sometimes assumed, groups are not a 'cheaper' alternative but have a far broader impact than an individual approach.

Fourth, when writing about how to manage violence in children, Dockar-Drysdale (1991) strongly indicated that unmanageable emotions in children must be managed by staff, and this we believe is the same when families are stuck in unhelpful or damaging situations. In Chap. 10, we describe a case study of a research project that suggested using a family worker in a mainstream school setting to ensure that children, parents and carers, and staff can all benefit from the dedicated time and space to address issues with mental health and well-being.

Fifth, it is often not just the child or young person who is in difficulty, but their parents too; sometimes with their own psychological issues but also their own perspectives on what is happening for their child. Parenting often means that people are faced with unresolved aspects of their own upbringing becoming stirred up. If not dealt with, these historical feelings can hinder their ability to see their child without the clutter of their own 'ghosts in the nursery' (Fraiberg et al., 1975).

Conclusion

This chapter has used a number of dilemmas for families and outlined how the practitioners thought about and approached the work. A key feature was opening and facilitating communication between parents and children. Not only did that shift parents' understanding of their child's feelings, but also, importantly, enabled them to have their own feelings recognised and held, too. Ideally, this would strengthen their relationship long-term, building trust that provides a solid foundation to address future challenges together.

References

Bacon, G., Sweeney, A., Batchelor, R., Grant, C., Mantovani, N., Peter, S., Sin, J., & Lever Taylor, B. (2023). At the edge of care: A systematic review and thematic synthesis of parent and practitioner views and experiences of support for parents with mental health needs and children's social service involvement. *Health and Social Care in the Community, 2023*(1), 1–23.

Boden-Stuart, Z., & Larkin, M. (2024). Conceptual foundations: Relational thinking for mental health contexts. In Z. Boden-Stuart & M. Larkin (Eds.), *Relationships and mental health: Relational experience in distress and recovery.* Palgrave Macmillan.

Cooper, A. (2018). The use of self in social work practice. In M. Bower & R. Solomon (Eds.), *What social workers need to know: A psychoanalytic approach* (pp. 109–123). Routledge.

Di Lorenzo, F., Barge, L., Thackeray, L., Peter, S., & Vainieri, I. (2023). More than I expected: A qualitative exploration of participants' experience of an online adoptive parent–toddler group. *Journal of Child Psychotherapy, 49*(2), 230–252.

Dockar-Drysdale, B. (1991). *The provision of primary experience: Winnicottian work with children and adolescents.* Jason Aronson Inc..

Fraiberg, S., Adelson, E., & Shapiro, V. (1975). Ghosts in the nursery: A psycho-analytic approach to the problems of impaired infant–mother relationships. *Journal of American Academy of Child Psychiatry, 14*(3), 387–421.

Gardner, F., Southall, A. E., & Baxter, L. (2022). Effectively supporting teachers: A peer supervision model using reflective circles. *Teachers and Teaching, 28*(3), 369–383.

Hill, R. (2025). *Raising confident teenagers: The take 3 approach to parenting calmly in a stressful world*. Karnac.

Midgley, N., Alayza, A., Lawrence, H., & Bellew, R. (2018). Adopting minds: A mentalization-based therapy for families in a post-adoption support service: Preliminary evaluation and service user experience. *Adoption & Fostering, 42*(1), 22–37.

Ogden, T. H. (1999). *Reverie and interpretation: Sensing something human*. Karnac.

Redgate, S., Smart, D., Barrett, S., Barron, C., Burns, S., Frost, H., McGovern, W., Peart, V., Adams, E., Alderson, H., Kaner, E., & McGovern, R. (2024). Mechanisms that promote and support family preservation for children at the edge of care: A realist synthesis. *Sage Open, 14*(2). https://doi.org/10.1177/21582440241260998

Selwyn, J., Wijedasa, D., & Meakings, S. (2015). *Beyond the adoption order: Challenges, interventions and adoption disruptions*. British Association for Adoption and Fostering (BAAF).

Taylor, S., Blackshaw, E., Lawrence, H., Stern, D., Gilbert, L., & Raghoo, N. (2023). *Randomised controlled trial of family group conferencing at pre-proceedings stage*. Retrieved January 29, 2025, from https://www.corum.org.uk/wp-content/uploads/2023/06/family-group-conferencing-report.pdf

CHAPTER 7

Supporting Staff

Dave Roberts and Heather Price

Introduction

What does supporting carers and staff look like in practice, and where do you start? There is no exact science about how to provide support as it is about developing a culture within an organisation. Supported staff and carers are then enabled to support the children and young people.

Pause for thought: Have you ever asked colleagues or your supporting network for a magical answer that you know doesn't exist, and then been disappointed that they haven't provided it? Or perhaps been cross that someone has said you are looking at things the wrong way? How important is the response you get from colleagues and from your wider team and your manager when you need to resolve a workplace problem? Ot, if you are a carer, the response coming from your peer support network or from other services?

Practice Example 1

These difficult emotions and thoughts will elicit similarly uncomfortable thoughts and feelings in the adult, which will trigger the adult's own past experiences. The child can then leave the unwanted thoughts and

C. Onions et al., *Supporting Children and Young People with Complex Needs*, Palgrave Texts in Counselling and Psychotherapy, https://doi.org/10.1007/978-3-032-16699-9_7

feelings behind for the other person to feel as if they were solely their own Some years ago, when Kae was running a residential home, things were feeling impossibly tough. The children seemed unable to be together as a group, mealtimes were horrible experiences, staff were getting hurt, and it all felt hopeless. Kae spoke with their supervisor/ line manager and was aware they wanted the manager to make it better, to do something magical that made it all okay. Instead, she challenged Kae as a leader, asking, 'when did you last bring the staff team together?' This seemed ridiculous. How could Kae hold a staff meeting when children were climbing out of windows and people were being hurt? But through reflection, Kae became increasingly aware that the child group were mirroring the experiences of the staff group, and that when the staff team were not working closely together the child group struggled to be together. The 'something magical' Kae wanted was within their control. Kae brought the staff team together twice weekly and focused on what was happening and the dynamics within the home. The team focused on how they were working together and whether individuals could be open and honest with each other. The children didn't suddenly cease having difficulties after this, but things became more manageable and could be discussed and worked with.

We all need different kinds of support in our settings. Hopefully, your workplace or your network supports you to be able to think through solutions to problems in a way that is validating but appropriately challenging, providing space for honest reflection. Perhaps you have a supervisor or a senior staff member or 'buddy' supporter you can genuinely trust and rely on for advice? If not, you may be keenly aware of what is missing in your organisation or network. There are costs to not having this, for you as an individual employee or carer, and for the child or children who need you to be 'on your game', as best you can be.

> Maybe reflective practices offer us a way of trying to make sense of the uncertainty in our workplaces and the courage to work competently and ethically at the edge of order and chaos. (Ghaye, 2000, p. 7)

This chapter explores the need for different kinds of reflective support and how vital access to it can be. It is easy to take the importance of staff or carer support for granted, and many organisations and services quite rightly include this as part of their job or placement offer. It is certainly rare for an organisation to say '*no, we don't support our staff and carers*', but underneath this lies a complex web of variable provision. What is needed depends on the client group that individuals are working with. It is clear is that no one model works for everyone, all the time. Staff or carer support is about developing a culture and resources across a workplace or service where people can explore what is needed and whether, and how, these needs can be met.

This chapter first looks at an Australian research study into therapeutic residential children's homes that emphasises the importance of wider systems of support. These can really affect the work on the ground. There is an inevitable limit to what an organisation can do about a lack of resourcing, responsiveness or direction, but it can, nevertheless be helpful to acknowledge and accept this. Accepting limitations then makes it possible to focus on changes that *are* possible.

We go on to explore the importance of emotional support for relationship-based practice through reflective practice. We introduce two examples showing how reflective support can help with the emotional impact of working with children and young people on the edge. One is from an adopter speaking about the importance of her support group, and one relates to the Mulberry Bush itself. These examples show how staff and carers might have to dig deeply and reflect on their personal lives and values in a way that is beyond what new staff and carers may initially expect.

Finally, we look at supervision. We outline what happened when group supervision was introduced for the first time in a special school that was part of an academy trust in Southeast England. This includes two further practice examples relating to supervision in a mainstream secondary school setting. We argue that supervision needs to be informed by a trusted theoretical model, such as a 'trauma-informed' approach, that makes sense of what everybody is experiencing on the ground. Some practical training in this model is needed to support practitioners and carers to feel competent and empowered in role. Unlike social workers, teachers, counsellors and psychologists, children's social care staff and teaching assistants often don't have professional training, and this is also true for foster and adoptive carers. Without a clear theoretical account that makes sense of why the children are responding the way they are, people can feel very exposed and vulnerable on the 'front line' during the day and perhaps especially at night when immediate support is less available.

Aims of the Chapter

This chapter

- considers how wider systems can affect the work on the ground;
- provides examples of how reflective practice supports an emotional 'coming to terms' with the impact of working with traumatised children and young people and
- shows how supervision supports practitioners, particularly those who do not have professional trainings as a resource.

The Impact of Wider Systems on a Residential Childcare Setting

In 2015, the Australian government launched an inquiry to address widespread allegations of the sexual abuse of children in a range of institutional settings, including children's homes and residential education (see the Australian Royal Commission, 2017). One outcome was the introduction of a therapeutic residential care model for the most traumatised children and young people placed in out-of-home care.

Kor et al. (2021), academics in universities in New South Wales, set out to research how well this new model was actually working in children's homes. They interviewed twenty-six practitioners working at different levels and in different roles in three in-state therapeutic residential care homes. As in the UK, Australian children's homes are small, typically containing four young people with complex behavioural needs and a team of direct care workers who, as in the UK, do not usually have graduate level professional training. The New South Wales homes were working to newly introduced therapeutic residential care principles—they used a 'trauma-informed' theoretical model, and for the first time, therapeutic specialists were employed to assess and place young people appropriately. The therapeutic specialists also supervised the direct care staff, whose rotas were thought about carefully so they could focus on engaging the young people and building relationships with them. There was also a big emphasis on inter-agency collaboration.

Kor and his colleagues found that although staff were committed to working in a trauma-informed way, it was not yet clear what this meant in practice, leading to inconsistencies and disagreements. The therapeutic specialists tended to emphasise moving away from a 'rewards and consequences' behavioural model. But the direct care practitioners expressed more unease about whether this was helping the young people face up to 'real world' consequences:

> The young person we've got at our house had heightened behavioural issues, they smashed the house completely, threw an apple at the television, it exploded, bit a staff member, kicked, spat at his face. And then that night, he got taken out to a movie. Would that happen in the real world if he was your child? (C, Direct Care Worker, in Kor et al., 2021, p. 4)

A big problem reported by staff was the crisis-driven nature of referrals. The assessors were under pressure to take young people quickly to avoid them being placed in unsuitable accommodation such as motels. They had to make quick placement decisions without really knowing enough about the young people. This led to children being placed together in homes in ill-matched ways:

> So, four kids walk in with, let's say only two different behaviours each. We're talking self-harm, assaults [...] these four kids blend. They walk out with an extra six behaviours. And that's just from this placement. They then walk into another placement, and they have only been in the care system for 18 months. And really, how are you meant to do good meaningful therapeutic work with all this noise going on? (M, Direct Care Worker, in Kor et al., 2021, p. 5)

In the interviews with staff, the authors of the study also heard how the emotional toll of the work, combined with poor pay and lack of recognition and career development opportunities, undermined their morale. This in turn could block the therapeutic care they were able to offer. One senior manager noted,

> When I'm reading incident reports, I'm seeing so much mirroring. If the team feels completely exhausted, the kids would be off the rails (T, Senior Manager, in Kor et al., 2021, p. 6)

Finally, the research study noted that supervision was not working well. There was uncertainty about whether the clinical supervisors should be based outside the children's homes or placed within them. There weren't enough supervisors for staff—sometimes there were only two or three clinical supervisors to forty or fifty staff members. One therapeutic specialist commented:

> Staff say, 'well you're not out here, you don't see the running of the houses, you don't see the kids, so how can you really make an accurate assessment?' I agree with them. I think we do need to have a clinical space that involves the clinician being at the house, observing the day-to-day running, providing on the ground clinical support to kids and staff members. (F, Therapeutic Specialist, in Kor et al., 2021, p. 7)

Overall, then, while the intention behind the introduction of therapeutic residential care in New South Wales was good, there were a lot of organisational and resource issues with the new model, and these affected the '24/7' work with the young people quite dramatically. The authors of the study concluded with a call for several changes to the new 'therapeutic residential care' initiative, including:

- clarifying the 'trauma-informed' practice framework;
- strengthening referral and assessment processes;
- providing better supervision and training to 'revitalise' the workforce and
- improving efforts at bringing staff together, from different professions and organisations.

Some of these recommendations might sound familiar in the UK, particularly the call for more collaborative working across systems; several clearly have resource implications. An individual children's home might have limited control over what can be changed in relation to the system it is working within. But there might be some autonomy in relation to how senior staff choose to define the trauma-informed practice model, to train their staff, and to develop and strengthen in-house supervision.

> *Pause for thought:* Are there quite significant limits in relation to how much control you and your team have over how you best care for the children and young people in your setting? Where might there be room for achievable change?

Support for the Emotional Impact of the Work

Those who have worked alongside children and young people will recognise that the emotional impact of the work on staff can be significant. Too often organisations fail to consider this impact with, understandably, the primary focus being on supporting the children and young people. Developing a culture of staff support needs careful thought and planning and, ironically, another problem that can get in the way of change is resistance and misunderstanding from the very staff we are trying to support.

Practice Example 2

I (Dave Roberts) remember when I had just started working at a residential special school and the director asked me how I was. '*Fine, thanks*' I answered without even really considering his question. He repeated his question for a second time and again I gave the same thoughtless answer. However, the third time he asked me I stopped and thought about his question and answered along the lines of '*I'm overwhelmed, out of my depth, the children don't like me and I have no idea what I'm doing here.*' These feelings were not simply about being new. Once I recognised how I really felt then I needed to do something about it. I needed some support—though that was also a new experience for me, as my social work training and previous employment undertaking case management had not prepared me for reflective practice that involved any deep level of self-scrutiny.

> *Pause for thought:* Does your organisation support staff to think about their own needs and feelings? Is this embedded in the culture of your workplace? If you are a carer, does your support network think about you and your emotional struggles, as well as the difficulties of the children in your care?

Being asked about feelings in a work or placement setting can feel completely new. To be honest, I thought it was really odd! We often ask children and young people how they are feeling, but the practice example above raises the potential for individual and cultural clashes in relation to asking people this 'personal' question. For many professionals or carers, talking about one's emotions and expressing these, particularly talking about problematic feelings like hate or inadequacy, is something of a taboo. People may wonder if it will indicate they are 'bad' or not coping. Or they may be left feeling uncomfortable or anxious, thinking, '*but it's the children's feelings that are causing the problem, not mine*!'

The development of personally reflective support structures across organisations is often thought to be a positive gesture—'staff will appreciate this'—but it often raises considerable anxiety. I have met with responses such as, '*You think I'm not doing a good enough job*', or '*Why are we talking about feelings? If I needed therapy I'd go to a therapist*', or '*What's wrong with how things are now?*' Yet these statements have all come from individuals who have said the work is having a huge impact on them, leaving them feeling overwhelmed, anxious and deskilled. The primary purpose of staff and carer support is to enable individuals and teams to undertake their work to the best of their ability. If they are overwhelmed or feeling deskilled, this doesn't happen.

Practice Example 3

Janice is a solo adoptive carer for a thirteen-year-old girl, Ava, who has emotionally based school avoidance (EBSA). Ava also regularly disappears in the evenings, changing phone settings so she cannot be tracked. Attempts at discussion about these issues usually descend into loud arguments, with Ava retreating to her room and slamming her door aggressively and repeatedly. Janice has referred Ava to different services and involved the police, but Ava is finding it hard to engage in any support. Four months ago, Janice herself was referred to a monthly therapeutic adoptive parents' support group that she was asked to commit to attending for a year. It is three hours long, run by two facilitators from CAMHS and social services, and has ten members. There is plenty of time for each parent to 'off-load' their feelings, and the focus is on mutual validation and support, and self-care. Parents also share how they have worked through some difficult experiences, but premature advice and solution-finding is discouraged. There is a parallel WhatsApp group for socialising outside the group and one-to-one linking if members wish to use this. Janice now has some more ideas about how to respond to Ava, but more importantly, she feels less alone and has a calmer part of herself she can draw on in the face of the 'storms' Ava generates inside her.

Pause for thought: What are your thoughts about a support group that is not focused on solution-finding, or practical advice and information about 'what works' for a particular problem (for example, EBSA)?

Not having solutions to what can feel like intractable dilemmas can be frustrating. But there is a lot of advice and guidance available online, or from trainings, discussing particular conditions or patterns of behaviour, and their possible causes. What is less accessible is ongoing personalised reflective support in relation to one's individual experiences with a particular child and how this affects one's own well-being and capacity to continue supporting in a compassionate and boundaried way.

While it is not the employer's or service's responsibility to offer therapy for staff or carers, a carer or staff therapeutic milieu or approach is different and can acknowledge the emotional impact the work has on individuals. Someone who is overwhelmed and goes off sick, or feels they can no longer support a placement, is of limited use to those with whom they work, or for whom they care. If we think of ourselves as a bucket that can contain a certain amount of stress, then, if we don't have a tap (our support structure that helps us process our feelings), our bucket will overflow. When that happens, the stress goes everywhere and is much harder to 'mop up' and manage (Fig. 7.1).

Reflective Practice at the Mulberry Bush

At the Mulberry Bush, all staff are required to attend regular group supervision, reflective spaces, one-to-one supervision and team meetings. They can expect to be in some of these spaces daily, some weekly, and some fortnightly. The focus in each space is on being able—indeed, expected—to say how one is feeling and what one thinks, regardless of who is in the group including more senior staff (to be able to 'speak truth to power', as one practitioner has put it—see Price et al., 2023, for a discussion).

Hawkins and Shohet (2012) suggest that even the most competent workers can be reduced to severe doubt about themselves and their abilities because of absorbing the emotional disturbance of the young people. A key concept frequently made use of at the Mulberry Bush is 'projection'. This is the psychodynamic idea that someone (for example, a child) may unconsciously use another (for example, a member of staff or carer) to put their difficult or unwanted emotions and thoughts into. These difficult emotions and thoughts will elicit similarly uncomfortable thoughts and feelings in the adult, which will trigger the adults own past experiences. The child can then leave the unwanted thoughts and feelings behind for the other person to feel as if they were solely their own. At the Mulberry Bush, this was described by a team leader as follows:

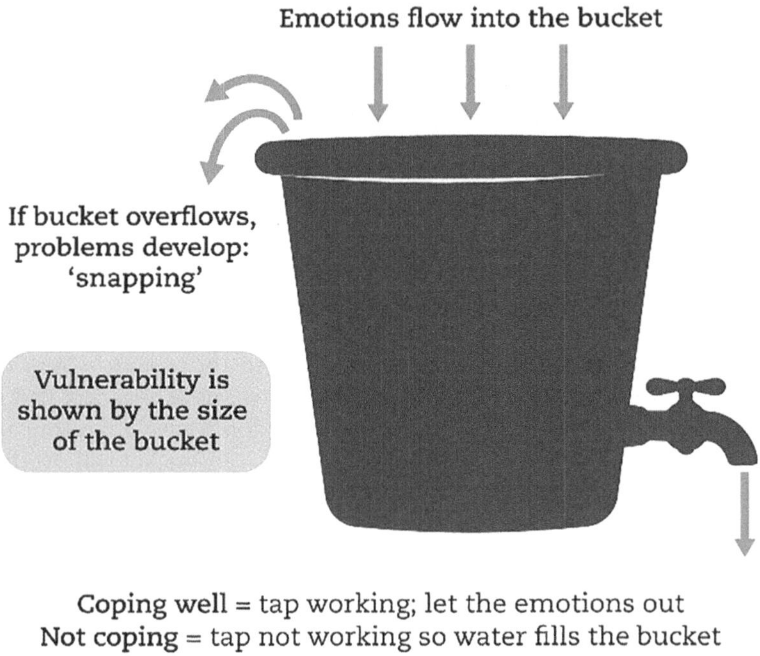

Fig. 7.1 Feelings bucket

> You have a feeling which you absolutely own, you go into your reflective space and you are a crap practitioner because you got it wrong with that child. The team support you to think about, let's have a think about what was going on for the child. Those feelings about feeling crap, yes, they're absolutely real for you, but what does that tell you about what was going on for—oh, okay so the child was feeling really crap. (Mulberry Bush House Manager, quoted in Price et al., 2023, p. 527)

Staff work closely in their teams to share the emotional impact of the work, to make sense of the children's communication and to process the impact of it, like a mother responding to and making sense of the distress of a baby, or a toddler having a tantrum. This reflective practice sits at the heart of the Mulberry Bush's culture of staff support, enabling staff to question their reactions and behaviours, as well as that of their professional peers, to improve practice and achieve greater understanding of the children's behaviour. Staff reflection allows projections to be recognised, understood and worked with, rather than purely felt.

In emphasising collaborative working, the Mulberry Bush also accepts that it is human to make mistakes in practice, to have vulnerabilities and old wounds, and to feel uncertain and to disagree with other people in your team. These trickier dynamics can lead to the potential for change, if the doubt and conflict they generate can be tolerated by the group. A facilitator of a reflective space spoke about it in this way:

> Quite often bickering can sit between two people around a particular child. But taking that into the group reflective space will often then result in somebody else going, oh do you know, that reminds me about the other day when so and so did such and such. You said that they could do that thing, and actually I was feeling a bit like, no! Then hopefully all of a sudden you have a team of people who are able to openly talk about differences in practice, how that feels, whether that's okay, can that be tolerated? Having a sense of agency in our work is really, really, important. (Mulberry Bush House Manager, quoted in Price et al., 2023, p. 530)

Pause for thought: In your work setting, or outside of parenting, do you have opportunities to reflect on yourself and the dynamics of 'what happened' after an event? If not, what would need to be changed to allow this to happen and what could you do to set the ball rolling?

Supervision

> When there is a crisis the first thing that gets cancelled is staff supervision, yet the first thing that is needed is staff supervision. (R. Rollinson, personal communication, 2001)

Like reflective practice, there are multiple definitions of supervision for professionals with specific definitions existing for different professions such as social work, health and counselling. This chapter uses a definition based on the work of Inskipp and Proctor (2001) and Scaife (2001), of supervision as:

> A working alliance which involves a formal arrangement where the supervisee can present an account of their work, reflect on it, and receive feedback, guidance, and support from a supervisor or peers. This collaborative process is designed to help the supervisee enhance their ethical competence,

confidence, compassion, and creativity. Ultimately, the goal is to provide the best possible service to clients while simultaneously fostering the supervisee's personal and professional development.

This working alliance, where one can receive feedback and guidance, includes what Hawkins and Shohet (2012) call 'helicopter ability', where supervisors may be able to stand back to help think about issues without holding the position of the line manager, or the expert, or what many people experience as 'judge and jury'.

Like reflective practice, this model of supervision is a protected regular space with an emphasis on what staff might learn from their experiences, through reflection, and how this can improve professional practice. It is an essential tool for protecting the emotional well-being of staff across settings. As noted above, we know that many staff and carers working alongside children, young people and families often feel overwhelmed and can absorb the intense projections as a barrage of raw emotions (see Chap. 3), which leads to high levels of staff absence, burn-out and, sadly, good staff leaving their roles (Watkins, 2020). Comprehensive staff support models, such as supervision, can help reduce all these, giving support in professional identity formation and providing some containment for the emotional impact of the work (Creaner, 2014). A further organisational benefit is the financial saving of improved staff retention and mental well-being.

However, it cannot be emphasised enough that supervision must be part of a culture, not seen as a 'bolt-on' in times of difficulty. Think of it as a garden plant—if you're not thoughtful about where you plant it, you will end up having to 'revive' the plant later, whereas if you plant it in the right place, with care and nurture it will grow into a culture that outlasts staff members.

Pause for thought: When you are left feeling overwhelmed within your work setting where can you go to for support, not for an answer?

Introducing Supervision Groups in a Special School

Willis and Baines (2018) have written about what happened when group supervision was introduced for the first time in a special school for primary-aged pupils with social, emotional and mental health needs (SEMH) and challenging behaviours. The school was suffering from low morale amongst its staff, with a lot of tension within and between teams. This threatened staff retention and contributed to staff sickness. Following a whole-school in-service training day looking at staff relations, the senior leadership team decided to introduce voluntary, externally facilitated, confidential group supervision. Staff could bring examples of their work and reflect together with the aim of improving staff relations and experiences of support. There were eventually three groups, each with five or six members, the majority of whom were teaching assistants.

In the original training day, staff had been introduced to one key psychodynamic concept and this was 'projective identification'. The trainer explained that staff supporting SEMH pupils are having to absorb unwanted aggressive and despairing projections every day. It becomes very easy to 'pass on' the projections to other team members: 'the emotional tone, affecting one and then another and another, appears to travel through the network like a ball on a pinball table' (Hinshelwood, 2001, p. 131). This concept was then used in the group supervision sessions to make sense of case material relating to supervisees' work.

Willis and Bains evaluated the new provision by interviewing twelve of the seventeen staff who took part. In their interviews with the researchers, the staff reported making productive use of the idea of 'projective identification':

> Am I seeing this situation as it is? Am I seeing the child and the difficulties they're having, or am I reflecting something onto the child, or am I taking on board what the child is [feeling]? It's helped me try to look at those kinds of relationships. (Supervisee K, in Willis & Baines, 2018, p. 270)

However, the most important finding was that the groups built staff camaraderie. They did this by providing opportunities to talk with different colleagues and to gain understanding, validation and empathy from other team members and to offer this in return:

> I feel it's definitely strengthened my relationship with members of staff in my group. I think it's made our relationships stronger. You look out for those people that are in your group. It makes a special bond. (Supervisee C, in Willis & Baines, 2018, p. 270)

An important additional benefit was that staff felt more able to cope with the stress of the work. One group member likened it to a massage. Another commented,

> Personally, it [supervision] helps me cope with the stress emotionally. It helps you to clear your mind, think a little bit more positively, and sometimes then go back and think, "Right, that's all gone. I've cleared that. I've spoken about that, so now I can almost start afresh". (Supervisee B, in Willis & Baines, 2018, p. 270)

The case study above focuses on the benefits of supervision in special schools, but Reid and Soan's work (2019) looked more broadly at mainstream school settings. They identified that, through supervision, staff felt themselves to be more reflective, more able to find their own solutions, had improved clarity of task and felt they saw the development of 'good' practice. Other researchers into supervision in schools have argued it leads to improved use of time and more constructive staff feedback, which shows that improved supervisory relationships can help staff, and therefore children, to feel valued, supported and motivated (Watkins, 2020; Wonnacott, 2012).

Practice Example 4

Lou, an executive head in a multi-academy trust, approached the Mulberry Bush to help introduce supervision to staff teams in four of the academy schools, to address high levels of stress, high absence and turnover. Lou had experienced supervision at a previous school and described it as being 'invaluable for thinking through what was going on, not just for the children but the staff team as well'. She had proposed to the four schools that they would benefit from supervision, and she explained she would be asking an external organisation to enable this. She would then leave it with the four headteachers to take things forward themselves. We offered to meet with the school leadership teams of each school to discuss, plan and perhaps give them an experience of supervision, but for logistical reasons this only occurred for two of the schools. We questioned whether the two we didn't meet with were committed to the new development.

Phase 1 of the project involved delivering individual supervision for thirty staff members, but only eighteen fully engaged. There was a mix of feelings and responses from curiosity, through mild apprehension to strong resistance. This was articulated through one teacher angrily saying 'so I'm in trouble again, am I? So, you're going to supervise my teaching and show me what to do, are you?' (remember Chap. 3's idea of behaviour as a communication—that happens for staff as well!). Another asked 'Why do I need supervision? Are you saying I'm not doing my job properly?'. It was noticeable that the two schools whose leadership teams were actively involved in setting up the project showed far more engagement, turning up on time, understanding the impact on the school and, for one team, even asking for additional supervision for their staff members.

One year later and both schools with engaged leadership teams have got into a pattern of monthly supervision; timetables have been adjusted so staff can be freed up for the sessions, staff are now being trained as supervisors themselves, and engagement is reported to be 'very good'. 95% of the scheduled supervisions have taken place and absence among the two schools with leadership engagement is lower than it has ever been. This has had a positive impact on the levels of cover staff needed, and the schools are described as 'more settled'. Meanwhile, in the other two schools, staff absence and behaviour issues with the children have both increased. Lou is currently looking at how to support the two 'resistant' leadership teams to help them see the benefits in the other schools and re-engage with supervision as a means of staff well-being.

Pause for thought: What would you require for supervision to be successfully introduced into your workplace culture? What assumptions might you and your colleagues make about new models of support being introduced?

As the practice example makes clear, for supervision to become an effective part of the staff support structure the model needs to be invested in by the senior leadership team. Without this buy-in, supervision will be a temporary support and fail to become an effective part of the support culture. An open dialogue is necessary to offer reassurance for staff anxieties, and ground rules need to be established. This dialogue typically covers the difference between supervision and coaching/mentoring and the role of establishing a supervision contract outlining the responsibilities for supervisee and supervisor. It emphasises that supervision is not just a space for 'moaning and dumping' but is informed by a trusted theoretical model that makes sense of what people are experiencing on the ground.

In some settings, staff have training on how to use supervision to support practitioners and carers to feel competent and empowered in role. However, we cannot ignore the challenges organisations may face. These can be real but can also be evidence of resistance. For example, ensuring regularity and releasing staff, even for an hour a month, can be enormously challenging but can also be offset by the improved staff well-being and attendance. Again, this is about developing a culture of staff support, and it is not a quick fix.

One key aspect that often needs clarifying is that supervision is **not** therapy (Scaife, 2019), but that supervisors may need to help the supervisee separate out those areas of the work that require discussion and supporting the development of practice from those that need to be explored, or resolved, outside of the workplace. For example, one staff member was struggling with their out-of-work relationship, which was clearly causing them stress. But supervision needed to be focused on the impact of their stress on their work, not on their external relationship.

A further area that often requires clarification is whether staff support is optional and available to everyone or not. In many professions, such as counselling or therapy, supervision is a requirement (BACP, 2023). Yet in education and care settings it is often seen as a luxury, or frowned upon, with people often relating supervision to poor performance. For our sectors to grow we need to move past these barriers and develop cultures of supervision across different settings, not just when there is a crisis but as a regular part of the working culture—we need to be more proactive, not reactive!

Conclusion

Throughout this chapter we have used practice examples and case studies to explore the importance of developing staff support structures as part of an organisational culture. Effective and well-embedded support structures enable staff to emotionally process the impact of the work with the children without becoming overwhelmed and experiencing burn-out. As such, reflective practice and supervision structures help form a protective layer for the staff team. Such support structures do not need to be resource-intense; instead, they require an organisational leadership commitment to developing a culture of support. If we look after our staff and carers, they will have greater emotional resilience and insight and therefore be more able to provide containment and care for the children.

The following chapter explores the benefits, and challenges, of collaborative working and how this can help us develop a deeper understanding of children's needs.

References

British Association for Counselling and Psychotherapy. (2023). *Supervision*. Retrieved July 30, 2025, from https://www.bacp.co.uk/membership/supervision

Creaner, M. (2014). *Getting the best out of supervision in counselling and psychotherapy: A guide for the supervisee*. SAGE Publications Ltd.

Ghaye, T. (2000). Into the reflective mode: Bridging the stagnant moat. *Reflective Practice, 1*(1), 5–9.

Hawkins, P., & Shohet, R. (2012). *Supervision in the helping professions* (4th ed.). Open University Press.

Hinshelwood, R. D. 2001. *Thinking about Institutions: Milieux and Madness*. London: Jessica Kingsley.

Inskipp, F., & Proctor, B. (2001). *Making the most of supervision. Part 1*. Cascade Publications.

Kor, K., Fernandez, E., & Spangaro, J. (2021). Practitioners' experience of implementing therapeutic residential care: A multi-perspective study. *Children and Youth Services Review, 131*, 106301.

Price, H., Brown, J., Herd, J., & Jones, D. (2023). 'A bit like you're going to therapy': Reflective practice provision at the Mulberry Bush School. *Residential Treatment for Children & Youth, 40*(4), 517–536.

Reid, H., & Soan, S. (2019). Providing support to senior managers in schools via 'clinical' supervision: a purposeful, restorative professional and personal developmental space. *Professional Development in Education*, 45(1), 59–72. https://doiorg.uwe.idm.oclc.org/10.1080/19415257.2018.1427132.

Royal Commission into Institutional Responses to Child Sexual Abuse. (2017). Retrieved July 28, 2025, from https://www.childabuseroyalcommission.gov.au/final-report

Scaife, J. (2001). *Supervision in the mental health professions: A practitioner's guide*. Routledge.

Scaife, J. (2019). *Supervision in clinical practice: A practitioner's guide* (3rd ed.). Routledge.

Watkins, C. E., Jr. (2020). What do clinical supervision research reviews tell us? Surveying the last 25 years. *Counselling and Psychotherapy Research, 20*(2), 190–208.

Willis, J., & Baines, E. (2018). The perceived benefits and difficulties in introducing and maintaining supervision groups in a SEMH special school. *Educational Review, 70*(30), 259–279.

Wonnacott, J. (2012). *Mastering social work supervision. London : Jessica Kingsley Publishers.*

CHAPTER 8

Keeping Children at the Heart of Collaborative Working

Mike Staines

Introduction

The challenges of caring for children with adverse histories sometimes means that insufficient thought is sometimes given to the other people who are part of the child's story, including families and professional networks. To effectively work with the difficulties a child or young person experiences, it is important we see them as part of a balanced system which can all too easily become disrupted. To effectively meet the needs of the child we need to consider the wider system and make sure the parts are working, and communicating, effectively together. This might sound straightforward but that is far from the case.

Practice Example 1

Sanjay sits in what he's been told is 'his' meeting. It's obvious to him that it's not his. A lady called Sian said she was 'chairing' (Sanjay notices she is wearing really big jewellery). Around the long, wide table are his mother (he knows she's upset and trying to look like she's not), his teacher (he wonders why she's wearing that suit today?), his dad (Sanjay wishes Dad would get off his phone), me (Sanjay has told me before

C. Onions et al., *Supporting Children and Young People with Complex Needs*, Palgrave Texts in Counselling and Psychotherapy, https://doi.org/10.1007/978-3-032-16699-9_8

that he doesn't like me being in the meeting 'cos his mum hates home managers), his foster carer (he's still not sure about her accent), his teaching assistant from class, Jo (he's glad Jo sat next to him, but Mum doesn't like that so he can't hold Jo's hand), his foster carer's social worker's manager (what?!), and his social worker (Sanjay likes that she's here this time, and hopes she doesn't annoy Dad today). The adults around the table take turns being angry about him, about everything and about each other…

Pause for thought: Have you been to meetings like this? What were your feelings and intentions before, during and after your meeting? What did your meeting achieve? Can you think clearly *how* that was achieved; what helped, enabled or allowed a group made up of family members, professionals and supporting stakeholders to work together?

When I was a keyworker and later when I managed a household team in a residential special school, I sat through dreadful meetings like Sanjay's review, but I also experienced meetings and networks that worked together effectively. In many of these meetings, what happened was predictable: a script was enacted by people who were pushed, pulled and held in roles by forces we did not talk about and were only partly aware of. I could see Sanjay's loyalties to each of his parents pulling him apart, while their sincere, passionate and different views on what he needed led them into a familiar tug-of-war that they probably both recognised yet appeared unable to avoid. Sanjay's mum, foster carers and Teaching Assistant (TA) all knew that everyone provided something good for him, but each struggled to move past their reactions to the other. For example, his mum's guilt and sense that she had failed him made the presence of other women who cared for him painful. This came out as cold politeness and picky criticism, leaving his TA bewildered and his foster carer exasperated. The TA went quiet and red in the face, while the foster carer became louder and looked at the ceiling while others spoke. These non-verbal, physical and bodily communications spoke loudly, but the rivalries and unprocessed feelings were unable to be shared openly. Each person was pushed and pulled by the complex relationships with all the others in the room, and a web of tension filled up the space that was meant to be used to think together about Sanjay. We each worked to be parental or professional.

Each of us could see Sanjay's discomfort and wanted to make him feel better, but his voice was the one we heard the least. We all wanted him to feel we were doing a good job, so people fought their corners and argued their points.

Aims of the Chapter

This chapter centres on the relational and interpersonal complexity of collaboration and how these can be described and worked through in practice. It draws on the treatment team model used in the Mulberry Bush school as well as the approach of Mulberry Bush consultation and training. Chapter 2 introduced the idea that we see collaboration as a way to achieve new understandings at the points where people meet, and that no one person's point of view takes precedence as the single and correct one. Chapters 3, 4, and 5 all contain examples of collaborative working towards a particular purpose. Using practice examples this chapter explores

- why working together is complex and challenging;
- how the challenges need to be worked with actively and constructively, and the importance of thinking about relationships;
- practical steps and structures to aid collaboration;
- the need to keep children central to collaboration; and
- applied systemic and psychodynamic principles.

Collaboration: An Old Idea that Proves Harder than Expected

Nobody puts forward the need to work in isolation. The recommendations made following the death of Victoria Climbié (Laming, 2003) are perhaps the best-known but were not the first to encourage better communication. For example, the inquiry into Maria Colwell's death in 1973 made recommendations 'designed to see that information is exchanged readily' (Committee of Inquiry, 1974, p. 19), and in 2015 the Quality Standards for Children's Homes (DfE) required children's social care staff to advocate for their children across professional networks. Collaboration, inter-agency working and interprofessional practice are central to policy, training and guidance for health, social care and children's services of all kinds. They consistently direct professionals to communicate as individual practitioners, to form multidisciplinary teams and to inhabit joint working structures (Crawford, 2012; Taylor & Thoburn, 2016). Collaboration is promoted as the key to early help, ensuring that professionals and those they support do not reach crises, such as the death of Baby Peter in 2007 (DCFS, 2009; HCPC, 2015; Taylor & Thoburn, 2016).

In the day-to-day reality of our work settings, working well with others has been and remains challenging (Moore & Zeeman, 2022; Cooper et al., 2024). Working Together to Safeguard Children (DfE, 2023b), which has the subtitle 'A guide to multi-agency working to help, protect and promote the welfare of children', has been substantially revised six times since it was first published in 1999. The NSPCC website lists recent Serious Case Reviews: after the first four months of 2025, the site listed sixteen summaries of reviews that all identify that information sharing and joint working could have and should have been better (NSPCC, 2025).

Practice Example 2

I am sitting with a colleague in a training room in a special school in the West of England during a reflective supervision course for the school's leadership team. The leaders, who are also trainees, today are taking turns supervising each other in groups. Jack, a teacher, is discussing Shula, a child in his class. Shula faces multiple complex daily challenges to access the school and engage in learning. Jack shares how hard he finds it that he cannot help Shula make more progress; he's losing sleep over it. He has done all the things he knows to do, used all the assessments available to him, and tried all the interventions both to the letter of the manual and more creatively. He has asked specialists in speech and language, occupational therapy and sensory needs to identify and reduce barriers to Shula's learning. His colleagues, who are also experienced special education teachers, validate his feelings and his approach, having also taught Shula in previous years. In fact, they used the same assessments, tried the same interventions and experienced the same slow progress in her learning and development. The trainee supervisor asks lots of probing questions: what form of a particular intervention was used? What resources are available that have not been tried? Was the classroom team all clear about the plan? The group repeats the same story a few times. When it is clear to everyone in the room that we are about to hear it again, with no new insights, I pause them.

We move people around. Now we have a facilities manager, a play therapist, an occupational therapist and a nurse in the group supervision exercise with Jack, who begins to repeat his long tale of failure. The facilities manager immediately cuts in and asks quite bluntly why Jack is doing the same things that his colleagues have done previously. Does he not trust them? Is he not respectful of their work? Why is he reinventing this particular wheel and wasting resources? Jack seems bemused and taken aback. He explains that he wants to make sure; to do his own assessments. The facilities manager is doubtful, head tilted, arms crossed. The occupational therapist comments that she sees this all the time: each year children move to new classes, and the new teacher starts again; she has to be pretty rude to get the new class teams to use the sensory aids and interventions already proven to be helpful and in the plan for the child. The play therapist chimes in now, and wonders if Shula has the capacity to learn any faster than she is and if she has better things to be doing. Her physical condition is likely to degenerate over the next few years; is the focus on educational outcomes appropriate to a child whose joy in physical movement and play may not last into adolescence, and whose life is likely to be shorter than many of her peers? This is painful—tissues are passed around, and a pause is taken. These people care deeply about Shula. The school nurse shares their experience on a children's ward, and how children who do not get better challenge the team's sense of purpose and identity. They talk about quality of life as a holistic thing made up of many factors. Jack is really struggling now, following his colleagues' conversation with a deep frown. The two therapists notice this and, after exchanging a brief glance, the play therapist says 'Jack, what you brought to supervision was your frustration that you couldn't achieve what you expect to achieve with Shula. In the end that's about you, your idea of failure or success as a teacher. What's right for her—it's surely not doing the things Jules and Koji have already done. Trust them…their work. You can focus on something else. Who knows, you might find things shift for other reasons…' The conversation carried on from here in this new direction so that both Jack's and Shula's needs could be disentangled and addressed.

Pause for thought: What do you think about the occupational therapist's comment that when children move up a year the things known to help them are often not implemented? Do you recognise this from transitions people make in your place of work—To a new doctor, children's home, class or social worker? How do you feel and think about the information people give you—Colleagues from your profession and different professions, stakeholders and children?

In Chap. 3, we thought about how your doctor not reading your patient file would impact you; now we are thinking about the doctor's motivations; their point of view. Being interested in our own and other people's points of view is key to collaborative working.

The example of Shula's teacher would be equally at home in the previous chapter on supporting staff. The supervision training Jack and his colleagues were enjoying draws on a model that uses self and role as a key focus (Rankine, 2017). The drives, professional cultures and identities of each of us working in services for children create blind spots and fixed habits of thought and practice (Moore & Zeeman, 2022). The Children's Social Care National Framework (DfE, 2023a, p. 32) asks us to 'work creatively, explore new ideas and initiatives to solve problems, and draw on the expertise of other agencies and professions to meet the needs of children, young people, and families'. To do this, we need to address our habits and blind spots, which is also a good definition of being reflective. A reflective culture is built on observation and feedback from other people (see Chap. 2); that is, on something collaborative. Collaboration, reflection and support are closely linked. They naturally come as a package, both as important concepts and in practice.

When we have collaborators who are in some ways unlike us, they are better placed to see and speak about the things we do not notice about ourselves. Jack would probably describe himself as dedicated and child-centred; however, a facilities manager sees ineffective repetition rather than due diligence. The four experienced teachers brought a wealth of expertise and were trying hard to be creative, but from only one point of view. Diversity of viewpoints is a key ingredient in any collaborating team (Syed, 2019). The play therapist was able to notice and speak to Jack's feelings about himself and about Shula. The therapist explored the complexity of Jack's personal investment in his professional identity in a way his fellow teachers could not. Genuinely different points of view shook things up helpfully, but it was uncomfortable. I imagine that Shula noticed she was being put through the same assessments and tasks and wonder how she felt about that. Fortunately, the perspective of the facilities manager brought this to our attention.

To think with others about ourselves in this way takes resources. We need time, space and energy for working collaboratively. We also require skills we gain through training and experience, like any other area of practice. Supervision is a structure intended for this work, but the trainee supervisor's stance, trying to problem solve and get into the details along established lines, reinforced existing habits and blind spots. The Mulberry Bush approach is to build and maintain a culture that can hold the tensions and debates intrinsic to collaboration with care and curiosity. The training scenario allowed me and a colleague to intervene with authority to set up a more diverse group, hold the resulting tensions, and validate and encourage contributions to the discussion that led to changes in self-perception. The focus on the wound to Jack's professional identity surprised the trainee supervisor and challenged his own practice both as a manager and a leader. It also made immediate sense to him; he could empathise with somebody in his own profession. The way we facilitated the situation, combined with the trainee supervisor's own openness, supported him to take the opportunity to combine his and other people's points of view and refine his practice as a leader and supervisor able to facilitate collaboration.

Practice Example 3

It is the coffee break between formal sessions of a training course in Therapeutic Childcare. Maryanna, a Senior TA working in a special school, is chatting about a child.

Most days, often before maths, eleven-year-old Zack reached his limits and was asked to take time out. Somewhere between his classroom and the time-out area something would happen that led to him being physically restrained. The restraint was always clearly justified as keeping Zack and others safe and preventing damage to the school. Each part of what happened focused on helping Zack, but nothing changed, and day after day the same script played out. Maryanna described the 'team around' Zack, comprising teacher, another TA, speech and language therapist (SALT), behaviour lead, learning support assistant (LSA), and the special educational needs coordinator (SENCO). She described how each of them was 'so committed' to helping Zack. A classmate asked her how they helped. Maryanna listed the aims and approaches of each of her colleagues. The classmate suggested that Maryanna wasn't describing a team so much as a group of people who happened to be working with the same child. Maryanna protested that they were a team; they had had many meetings trying to fit together all the possible ways to help Zack. The classmate asked if those people were 'experts in Zack?' Maryanna said they all wanted to help. The classmate said he had not asked if they wanted to be helpful but if they had expertise in helping Zack. 'I am…not the expert…he likes me.' Her classmate asked 'Could you get him through the day without being physically held?' Maryanna said she could get him from the classroom to somewhere he could calm down. When the classmate asked what stopped her, Maryanna described all the transitions during the day that made it harder for Zack. These were mostly transitions to and from interventions and people coming and going to help in different ways. Maryanna's classmate said, 'The boy doesn't need all that—you need a team who have your back, and Zack needs you to get him through. And you need one target for Zack, not a shopping list.' Maryanna was doubtful about some of this, but her classmate convinced her: 'Tell them they are not actually helping!'

Six weeks later, Maryanna shared that things were improving. She said it had taken a huge amount of 'time, bribery and arm-twisting', but she had managed to get most people to sign up to one purpose, which was getting through a day without using a physical intervention with Zack. Her notepad is shown in Fig. 8.1. There had been setbacks when Zack had managed a day without a hold then been physically held twice the next day, or damaged something while Maryanna tried to guide Zack to a calmer place without resorting to a hold. The team had been wobbly for a while each time this happened.

Maryanna described how each person had taken some kind of risk, which had allowed other people to feel more able to take good risks. Something had shifted that had been stopping effective collaboration. Maryanna linked this strongly to trust.

After the school's caretaker, Zen, had had a cup of tea with Maryanna, they agreed to have a cup of tea and a biscuit with Maryanna and Zack. Maryanna invested further cups of tea and chat persuading Zen that sticking to their zero-tolerance-for-damage would mean zero chance the damage being caused to the school building would stop. As a result, the caretaker stopped complaining loudly about Zack's behaviour. In fact, when they did have tea and a biscuit together, the caretaker took a liking to Zack. Zack has started helping the caretaker keep the school tidy when he's out of class. Then Zack's teacher gave the caretaker ideas for counting and time telling games. They count bins and black bags, time themselves mopping floors and talk about when it's time for a tea break. Zen has agreed to go along with this but says they don't get paid to do the teacher's job for them. Meanwhile, Maryanna felt able to take

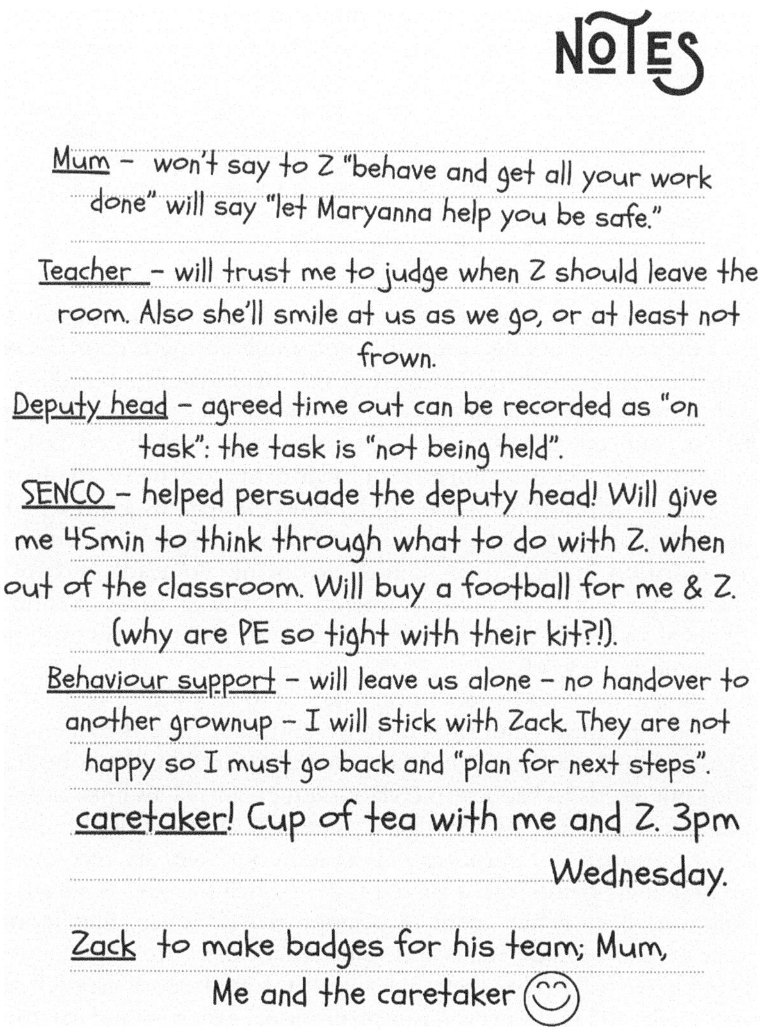
NOTES

Mum – won't say to Z "behave and get all your work done" will say "let Maryanna help you be safe."

Teacher – will trust me to judge when Z should leave the room. Also she'll smile at us as we go, or at least not frown.

Deputy head – agreed time out can be recorded as "on task": the task is "not being held".

SENCO – helped persuade the deputy head! Will give me 45min to think through what to do with Z. when out of the classroom. Will buy a football for me & Z. (why are PE so tight with their kit?!).

Behaviour support – will leave us alone – no handover to another grownup – I will stick with Zack. They are not happy so I must go back and "plan for next steps".

caretaker! Cup of tea with me and Z. 3pm Wednesday.

Zack to make badges for his team; Mum, Me and the caretaker

Fig. 8.1 Maryanna's notepad

some risks with Zack herself, trying different things rather than moving through the familiar doom loop when he was struggling and needed to leave the classroom.

Pause for thought: Have you been in situations where you didn't feel able to do things because you didn't feel authorised or trusted? What did you do in that situation?

Collaboration is not simply everyone doing their work in the way they would if they were working alone; it is not simply fitting everyone's work in neatly. Sometimes the right person or role needs room to work on the thing that needs attention first. The best use of our resources can be in support of someone else's work, or some aspect of a shared task that doesn't directly achieve the purpose our role exists to achieve. Many practitioners in the helping professions understand the systems around people. It is no longer innovative to see how working on a family's housing situation or nutrition impacts their mental well-being alongside perhaps the play therapy session we are commissioned to provide. It is easy to find our roles blurred and shifting in a collaborating team. This involves both practical and emotional work.

Most people working therapeutically or relationally will be familiar with the idea of regulating emotional distance and managing the intensity of the relationship (Diamond, 2003) and thinking carefully about boundaries. The same needs to happen in collaborating teams. This links closely to a sense of safety. When we feel heard, understood and thought about—when our priorities and purposes as people in our roles are recognised—we can genuinely commit to a shared task in a helpful way, as a leader, or as a follower, as an active agent or a supportive presence. Furthermore, when we genuinely understand and value what others are doing, and feel safe enough, we will likely experience a healthy impulse to assist each other (Cooper et al., 2024). However, our professional expertise and experience is the reason we are there to collaborate and is something others cannot provide (Weller et al., 2014; Bevington & Fuggle, 2012). Issues of authority and authorisation will arise and need to be given attention. Maryanna's deputy head holds others accountable for being on task and this remains their role, so their agreement and understanding of the goals being set is key to the project, and having this shared understanding in place empowers those working closely with Maryanna and Zack. Zack's teacher may well feel both anxiety and relief at Maryanna's assertiveness, which inverts the hierarchy of teacher and TA to one based on 'Zack expertise'. However, they remain the teacher, accountable for attainment and achievement. They seem prepared (skilled enough and safe enough) to do this creatively, working via the caretaker to keep an eye on Zack's progress in maths. The caretaker also seems prepared for role blurring but has a point in that they are not being paid and are not trained to be a TA or a teacher, while their contribution here is clearly helpful and likely rewarding.

What is happening in Maryanna's and Zack's teams fits well with ideas about creating a therapeutic system around the child even though we are not therapists.

Being Minded to be Helpful

A key psychodynamic understanding is that we all need to be thought about and to have our true selves recognised. When we aim to help a person through relationships, by talking with them, living alongside them, or teaching them, we must have space for them in our minds (Barratt & Kerman, 2001; Freeman, 2016). This also applies to those with whom we need to collaborate. Furthermore, therapy, care, social work, looking after, teaching and training are all collaborative processes. We do not do these things *to* people; we do them *with* people. Collaborative relationships are dialogues: they take at least two. We try to hold others in mind as people, not just in their roles and, conversely, we need to be open to being held in mind as a person ourselves. I am not suggesting a traumatised child, her GP, social worker, teacher and counsellor should drop who they are and become a group of peers without differentiation; not at all. Nor that children receiving help should be looking after the professional providers of that help. I am suggesting that we need to be present as people in our roles, and that working on *how* we are present as people is integral to effective collaboration. Jack had lost track of both himself and Shula as whole persons, as he was committed to a narrow purpose of Shula learning more, and more quickly. If he had been thinking holistically about Shula, and had more space in his thoughts for her as a whole person rather than a problem to solve, he might have been able to change course somewhat sooner. He might at least have asked her opinion, to incorporate her perspective. When Maryanna and her classmate talked about 'Zack expertise', I thought they were talking about this quality in their relationship; each can mentalise (Freeman, 2016) the other and they have a partnership. Her hard work expanded this to other relationships.

It is important to distinguish this kind of *thinking together* from *being together but thinking separately* and from insisting everyone thinks the same. As noted in Chap. 2, collaboration is therapeutic when we grapple with things together, each contributing their own perspective but allowing new understandings to emerge.

In Sanjay's review, everybody was thinking about Sanjay—at least, we were each thinking about our version of what would help him. Each of us was preoccupied by what we felt we should do to feel we were being helpful—just like Jack in relation to Shula. If Sanjay was going to be helped, we needed to think together. One way to say this is that the team collaborating to help Sanjay needed to be of one mind. Not one thought, as a healthy mind can hold different thoughts, doubts, tensions and can change its opinion, but we needed to be a joined-up mind that had Sanjay's experience at the centre of its attention. Collaboration requires shared mental models and a team identity alongside good role demarcation, open and informal communications, and mutual respect (Atkinson et al., 2007; Weller et al., 2014). Everyone in Sanjay's review needed to mentalise the others in order to build a healthy 'us' in our minds and in practice. We might then have been able to combine our various understandings of Sanjay and hold him in mind together.

Building a new 'us' involves paying attention not only to the push and pull of forces between and within professional teams, but also between professionals and the recipients of services (children on the edge of care, residents, patients, clients) and other stakeholders (family members, advocates, community members and leaders). Developing an 'us' means collectively acknowledging our different views and perspectives and working with them in the same way as Jack needed to acknowledge his individual habits and blind spots. This includes thinking about our identities. Our new collaborative identities are likely to challenge or compete with those we are loyal to and relatively safe within (Moore & Zeeman, 2022). If we are part of a team, profession or workplace, we will probably have a few groups with whom we already strongly identify. With these ingroups will inevitably come some outgroups who we define ourselves as different from; 'theys' to our 'us'. The people we are trying to collaborate with are often part of our theys; nurses are not patients, adults are not children, staff are not residents.

Perhaps the challenge becomes clearer if we talk of sharing power, flattening hierarchies, allowing others to do our job, letting go of hard-earned responsibility and status, blurring our identity, working on implicit biases, and risking being vulnerable in front of 'them'. If Sanjay was going to be helped, we needed to think together *including with Sanjay.* We have already noted what Jack could have gained from talking with Shula.

> *Pause for thought:* Think about your professional role. What privileges and responsibilities come with that identity? Where, when and by whom are you taken seriously and listened to? Who or what are you accountable to? If you were collaborating with people in different roles and professions, would your answers change?

In building a healthy team things like Maryanna's tea and biscuits are crucial. We place great value on informal time together, when we create relationships between ourselves as people as well as roles. Note that we may all perform and protect a role, even if that is a personal role such as 'Sanjay's mum', rather than a professional role, such as 'Sanjay's social worker'. Time spent together means we come to understand how and why people think as they do, so we move towards both knowing each other better and being closer to one mind. Formal structures, such as scheduled reflective groups and group supervisions, are very effective but are closely tied up with established roles, who holds power, who knows what and who can make decisions. Informal time together will feed good things into formal structures as relationships between roles are supplemented with relationships between people, assumptions are challenged and our mental sketches of each other are filled out and come closer to the actual person.

Back in 1974, the committee inquiring into Maria Colwell's death knew that 'face-to-face contact on a regular basis creates an entirely different situation' and that 'unless the men and women concerned have confidence in each other' things would go wrong (Committee of Inquiry, 1974, p. 19). Contemporary modern research places just as much weight on 'co-located teams' (Taylor & Thoburn, 2016, p. 9). Sanjay's reviews were better after his keyworker and I visited his dad at home, and much better after his mum and her partner visited. She lost her phone charger, and we spent an hour trying to find it only to realise I'd put it in my pocket. She teased me about this every time we spoke for the rest of

Sanjay's time living with us. Informal moments of humour help us get in touch with each other's reality.

In the discussion of Shula's teacher, we noted that working on collaboration as we are describing it requires investment. Thought needs to be given to resources alongside relationships.

'Sounds Great, Shame I Don't Have Any of That Available!'

Too often we hear individuals and organisations comment that they cannot meet the needs of a child or young person due to a lack of resources. While there may be some reality to this, often what is needed is a mindset shift. What can we do with what we do have?

Practice Example 3

Zack, who we met earlier, was adopted aged one. His adoptive mum, Sasha, and her husband, knew that a child in need of adoptive parents might have had a complex life so far and the details of Zack's early trauma were shared with the family. Sasha was not ready for how hard it proved to be when Zack didn't respond to things the way other children did. She sought support from social services, her GP and from anyone she thought might help. She told Maryanna, 'There's nobody there who's meant to help—who I could just talk to, just say things and feel heard and get some space to think. When it all gets too much, you get offered a few parenting classes, and if things are really bad, it's respite, but they let you know you're doing something wrong. Meanwhile…it's like you have to be failing…a "risk" (Sasha makes speech marks with her fingers and grimaces) to be noticed, not a good mum struggling. They don't see *you*!' Sasha slowly built a network for her family, finding people who understood; a nurse at the GP surgery, her sister's husband who was great with Zack, neighbours who would pick him up from school if he wasn't coping when Sasha was working. Once Zack was diagnosed with Foetal Alcohol Syndrome Disorder, things were a bit easier, but Sasha finds it hard having to 'scratch about for help.'

> *Pause for thought:* What resources do you have available to you in your helping role? What are you grateful for? What do you struggle with?

The obvious resources needed for collaboration include people to reflect and collaborate with; time to do things (meet, talk, relate, reflect); time for things to happen (trust to build, relationships to strengthen, thinking to align), and physical space for all this to happen in. Less tangible resources are crucial. These include permission. Permission from ourselves in our roles, from managers and supervisors, from friends and family around those needing help. Permission to have feelings, take risks, express vulnerability, build connections. We need internal resources—energy, courage, hope, knowledge—alongside permission and external, concrete resources.

In many workplaces, organisations and roles, and in many lives and families, these resources are lacking. On our Mulberry Bush courses and trainings we often hear people say, 'This all sounds great. I don't have that kind of time and I don't work in that kind of place.' There is no one solution to this, and the political and systemic changes needed to enact widespread change across the provisions for children on the edge of school and family is beyond the scope of this chapter. What is important is that differences in and tensions around resources are acknowledged and discussed like any other aspect of collaboration—reflectively and with respect. Differences in resources can get in the way of relationships as much as any other kind of difference. Professionals can be seen as gatekeepers, hoarding resources that are desperately wanted. However, one of the benefits of collaborative working is sharing resources, and much of what is crucial to collaboration doesn't need some of the more tangible resources, although time is important and needs accounting for. Informal time together doesn't require a formal space. We can think about each other as long as we have the energy to do so. What one professional or service lacks another may have. It can be incredibly hard work, particularly for parents, carers and other non-professionals, but Sasha, and Maryanna, constructed the collaborative teams they needed.

We also need to do regular maintenance on our collaborations.

Keeping on Collaborating

Once we have collaboration working well enough, it must be maintained, otherwise things go backwards. Key to this is remaining open, honest and reflective with our collaborators. There will always be moments of doubt and anxiety when we seek to help children on the edge of school and family. The various professional 'tribes' (Weller et al., 2014) and stakeholder identities (Crawford, 2012) are likely to clash and argue over control, territory and priorities. At those times individuals will create a sense of safety for themselves by retreating to familiar positions and interactions if their relationships with collaborators are not secure enough (Moore & Zeeman, 2022). For example, if Zack's teacher anxiously pushes the caretaker too hard to do maths (the maths Maryanna would be doing with Zack if he were able to stay in the classroom) and the caretaker feels resentful or overwhelmed they may decide to stick to their job description. This retreat to role may spread through the system and things would be at risk of going backwards.

Conclusion

Our roles are to help people. Therefore, if collaboration is to be effective, we need to

- value being with people who are different from us who can point out our habits and blind spots, as well as appreciate our strengths;
- keep the people we are trying to help at the centre, as being a good team is not an end in itself;
- recognise that collaboration, particularly with those we see as 'needing our help' or 'holding less responsibility' involves both holding our roles clearly and at the same time being prepared to let them go;
- acknowledge the resources our collaborators have, share, and live within our means and
- commit time, space, energy and training to reflect on what we are doing. This means spending time together allowing others to know us, and getting to know them, beyond their role.

References

Atkinson, M., Jones, M., & Lamont, E. (2007). *Multi-agency working and its implications for practice*. Reading: CfBT Education Trust. Retrieved June 11, 2025, from https://www.nfer.ac.UK/publications/multi-agency-working-and-its-implications-for-practice-a-review-of-the-literature/Multi-agencyWorkinganditsImplicationsforPractice:Areviewoftheliterature-NFER

Barratt, G., & Kerman, M. (2001). Holding in mind: Theory and practice of seeing children in groups. *Psychodynamic Counselling, 7*(3), 315–328.

Bevington, D., & Fuggle, P. (2012). Chapter 9: Supporting and enhancing mentalization in community outreach teams working with hard to-reach youth. The AMBIT approach. In N. Midgley & I. Vrouva (Eds.), *Minding the child: Mentalization-based interventions with children, young people and their families.* Taylor & Francis Group.

Committee of Inquiry into the Care and Supervision Provided in Relation to Maria Colwell. (1974). *Report of the Committee of Inquiry into the care and supervision provided by local authorities and other agencies in relation to Maria Colwell and the co-ordination between them* (Chairman: T. G. Field-Fisher). Her Majesty's Stationery Office.

Cooper, Z. W., Johnson, L., Washington, T. R., & Lewinson, T. (2024). Analyzing the roles, workflows, and communication dynamics of social workers within interprofessional care teams. *Journal of Interprofessional Care, 38*(6), 1016–1025.

Crawford, K. (2012). *Interprofessional collaboration in social work practice.* SAGE.

Department for Children, Schools and Families. (2009). *The protection of children in England: A progress report.* Retrieved June 16, 2025, from https://assets.publishing.service.gov.uk/media/5a7eb005e5274a2e8ab478fb/The_Protection_of_Children_in_England.pdf

Department for Education. (2015). *Guide to the Children's Homes Regulations including the quality standards April 2015.* Retrieved June 14, 2025, from https://assets.publishing.service.gov.uk/media/5a7f1b54ed915d74e33f45f0/Guide_to_Children_s_Home_Standards_inc_quality_standards_Version__1.17_FINAL.pdf

Department for Education. (2023a). *Children's social care national framework.* Retrieved June 15, 2025, from https://assets.publishing.service.gov.uk/media/657c538495bf650010719097/Children_s_Social_Care_National_Framework__December_2023.pdf

Department for Education. (2023b). *Working together to safeguard children.* Retrieved June 15, 2025, from https://assets.publishing.service.gov.uk/media/6849a7b67cba25f610c7db3f/Working_together_to_safeguard_children_2023_-_statutory_guidance.pdf

Diamond, J. (2003). Organic growth and the collective enterprise. *Therapeutic Communities, The International Journal for Therapeutic and Supportive Organisations, 25*(3), 169–184.

Freeman, C. (2016). What is mentalizing? An overview. *British Journal of Psychotherapy, 32*(2), 189–201.

Health and Care Professions Council. (2015). Preventing small problems from becoming big problems in health and social care. HCPC. Retrieved June 21, 2025, from https://www.hcpc-uk.org/resources/reports/2015/preventing-small-problems-from-becoming-big-problems-in-health-and-care/

Laming, W. H. (2003). *The Victoria Climbié inquiry: Report of an inquiry by Lord Laming* (cm 5730). The Stationery Office.

Moore, T., & Zeeman, L. (2022). A psychosocial exploration of resistances to service user involvement in United Kingdom National Health Service (NHS) mental health services. *Health, 27*(6), 1096–1114.

NSPCC. (2025, April 17). *Recently published case reviews.* NSPCC Learning. Retrieved May 26, 2025, from https://learning.nspcc.org.uk/case-reviews/recently-published-case-reviews

Rankine, M. (2017). Making the connections: A practice model for reflective supervision. *Aotearoa New Zealand Social Work, 29*(3), 66–78.

Syed, M. (2019). *Rebel ideas: The power of diverse thinking*. Hachette.

Taylor, J., & Thoburn, J. (2016). *Collaborative practice with vulnerable children and their families* (1st ed.). Routledge.

Weller, J., Boyd, M., & Cumin, D. (2014). Teams, tribes and patient safety: Overcoming barriers to effective teamwork in healthcare. *Postgraduate Medical Journal, 90*(1061), 149–154.

CHAPTER 9

Leavings and Endings

Caryn Onions

Introduction

Many children on the edge of home and school life will have had sudden and unplanned endings and perhaps little experience of a good, coherent and meaningful goodbye. This is a big theme for all children, whether they are moving up a year, leaving school, or leaving care and becoming 'independent'. In fact, these endings are around us all our lives and each one helps us prepare for the next, or not. This chapter explores leavings and endings and how we help children and staff say goodbye. It is also about why people avoid endings and the painful aspects of endings. You might want to look back at Chap. 3, on new beginnings. The chapter ends with the voices of two care experienced adults and their reflections on accessing their care records.

Practice Example 1

Josie had been at the Mulberry Bush for three years and today was her last day. At her leaving assembly she sat at the front facing the other pupils. They were sitting cross-legged on the floor in front of semicircles of chairs where she could see the staff, her social worker, and her foster parents smiling at her encouragingly. Everyone was chatting, the energy was high, and her friends were shouting out to her; she had butterflies

C. Onions et al., *Supporting Children and Young People with Complex Needs*, Palgrave Texts in Counselling and Psychotherapy,
https://doi.org/10.1007/978-3-032-16699-9_9

in her stomach. The head stood next to her and put his hand on her shoulder, and the room quietened as he read out some memories and anecdotes that had been written about her time at the school. After the head had finished friends and staff came up and gave Josie a photograph album, handmade cards and a blanket. As it was draped over her shoulders the head suggested that in the future, she could wrap herself up in the blanket and have warm memories of her time at the Mulberry Bush.

Pause for thought: Think about endings that you have been involved with, perhaps your own or that of a child you have worked with. Was it a positive experience or could it have been done differently?

At the Mulberry Bush, when a child leaves, the process starts quite a while before their actual last day. Children plan activities with staff and friends who have been significant, to help them say goodbye to important relationships and look back and reflect on their time together. The leaving process culminates in a dedicated leaving assembly where we all say goodbye to the person. This ritual probably started in the 1970s and has been developed to give the children and staff a planned and nurturing experience of leaving. Many have had previous unplanned and sometimes traumatic endings, and nowadays we consciously give the children a different experience; one where we can say thank you to people who have helped us, as well as allowing ourselves to feel sad that their time has come to an end. There is also an aspect of hope and looking to the future and we want to bring in all these aspects to help children see that endings, although difficult, can be tolerable and even helpful.

Practice Example 2

This is what Kai, aged fifteen, said when he found out that his teacher Mike was retiring from his special day school.

> I was gutted when I heard that Mike was going, brought tears to my eyes. I know he looks older than the rest, but I didn't think he'd leave before me. He was like an uncle to me, could tell him anything! We used to have a laugh at lunchtimes, and he even talked me down from the roof when I got heated once. He used to chat with my dad on parents' evenings—he liked

him, he did. He wasn't a push-over, but he said it like it was. Maybe he'll come round to ours sometimes when he leaves.

Kai was devastated when he heard that Mike was retiring; he stormed off across the field and lashed out at a bush. He didn't want anyone to see him crying but he also wanted Mike to know how much he would miss him. Kai had been in a special school since he was eleven and Mike had become the adult Kai trusted the most. Mike had talked Kai down off the roof more than once, helped him feel safe enough not to bring a knife into school, and helped his dad after his mum left them for another man. Mike seemed to understand Kai's moods and managed to find the right thing to say. Colleagues often said that it was their bond that helped Kai feel like he belonged at the school and be relaxed enough to sit in a class and learn. Staff were all too familiar with Kai's explosions and were also concerned how they would manage when Mike left. Endings like these can trigger previous losses, and Kai and his dad were easily brought back to the time when they were 'abandoned' by Kai's mum. Mike had been with them during that time and knowing how painful it had been for them really helped Kai manage his rage. There was a time when he was fiercely jealous when any other children mentioned their mums and wanted to lash out at them, which he did a couple of times. Mike's own mother had died when he was a teenager, and he was able to recognise similar feelings and behaviour and used his own experience to gently open the conversation with Kai. Initially Kai felt embarrassed and denied what Mike said, but he also realised that Mike was being kind and not teasing him. Kai had taken his mother's sudden departure from the family as evidence that he was a terrible son, plus he didn't know that his parents had been having difficulties for years as his dad wasn't a 'talker'. Mike didn't say too much about his mother's death, but enough to let Kai know that he was not alone and that these things happen and that people can eventually get on with their lives.

Pause for thought: Have you ever left a job and been worried about a child you've worked closely with? Have you ever experienced a difficult or unsatisfying end to a job or the loss of someone you cared for at work?

A common feature of many children on the edge of school and home life is unresolved loss, often loss within the family context. The impact of these accumulated unresolved losses is that other endings may seem scary and too much to bear. For example, in Chap. 4, you read about Samina, who was leaving a children's home and moving to foster carers and in Chap. 6 about Emily, whose father took his own life. In both practice examples, the underlying reason for the child's distress turned out to be the loss of a significant relationship that had not ended well or was, for Emily, a devastating shock.

This chapter looks at some theories about what makes endings tricky for children and staff as well as endings where things feel more bearable and appropriate.

Aims of the Chapter

- To highlight theory relating to the feelings that children, young people and adults might have when they leave a setting, or when a relationship with an important person ends;
- To demonstrate how early experiences shape a person's reactions to change and transition;
- To consider how we, as practitioners, might develop systems and processes to support transitions for children and young people and staff and carers; and
- To explore the experience of accessing care records.

Do we Take Endings Seriously Enough?

Why are endings so difficult and how come some students drift off unnoticed, bunk off the last day of term, seem to try and mess up their placement endings and generally avoid saying goodbye? The profound feelings of loss and sadness that people grapple with might mean that it is easier to minimise goodbyes or even avoid endings altogether. Salzberger-Wittenberg (2013) puts it very clearly:

> Most teachers care deeply about their groups, miss pupils they have become especially fond of and those whom they have helped through difficult times, witnessed their growth, taken pleasure in their achievements. And yet what teachers and students feel about each other is not given space to be expressed and worked through: neither the anger at failure nor the resentments are

faced but remain as unfinished business. But neither are gratitude, acknowledgement of good experiences they shared, nor sadness at parting addressed. Seeing that the teachers do not speak about how they feel about the relationship coming to an end, students tend to assume that their teachers don't care that much about them. What a sad situation, what a missed opportunity to learn that it is possible to part in a good, appreciative way (p. 75)

The quote is equally valid in all other situations where young people might need to say goodbye, but what might be going on in their minds? Here are some possible thoughts and feelings that may be occurring at the same time

- anger with the person for leaving, as anger is generally easier and more tolerable than sadness;
- disconnecting and becoming emotionally distant from the person;
- regressing to younger child behaviours;
- denigrating the old and idealising the new;
- inaccurate imaginings about the cause of the ending and overvaluing one's part in it; and
- attempting to keep things going and denying the ending.

To acknowledge that you will be sad and miss the teacher, friend, foster carer or mentor means that you need to recognise those feelings and have words to describe them, and that might not be easy, especially for young people where feelings seem unsafe and have not been talked about. It also leads people to wonder whether they will be missed. Look back at Chap. 5 and see what was written about helping children express strong feelings.

Young people leaving residential settings are especially vulnerable when things come to end. In 2024, 33,620 children left the care system, an increase of 10% since 2014 (Department for Education, 2024). Children in residential care will not have been living with their families, and many will have experienced upsetting and painful endings, often where conflicts are left unresolved and hanging. In addition, they are likely to have had lots of different moves within the care system. One pupil who left the Mulberry Bush in the 1970s said this about their experience:

I personally felt that leaving the school was a huge bereavement. It felt like losing your whole family, your tribe. Knowing that everyone was still there but the door was shut to you really hurt. It created a huge fear of the

> unknown and knowing that the support network was no longer there was very hard to deal with. It made it harder to bond with new carers and social workers. It recreated mistrust.

We are pleased to say that practice has changed since the 1970s, when practitioners thought it would help children make a better start at their next school or home if there was a clean break. However, as we wrote in Chap. 3, transitions are especially difficult for children with complex lives, and the Break Staying Close, Staying Connected Project was initiated to research this all too familiar and sad situation in the UK (Dixon et al., 2020). Recognising that young people leaving residential care do not have the same opportunity to stay put as those in foster care, the project helped young people keep in contact with someone from their residential setting, plus they allocated a 'transition worker' to young people leaving care who supported them throughout their Staying Close journey (Dixon et al., 2020, p. 9). The voice of the participants suggests that they want to feel safe and they like the idea of transition homes. The young people also wanted more timely support when making decisions and help to feel better prepared for housing and finances. Attachment to places, things, routines, as well as people is what makes us feel safe and secure (Bowlby, 1980) and is at the heart of what care leavers need as they mature and move towards adulthood.

These examples could be said to be at either end of the scale: at one end, the Salzberger-Wittenberg quote refers to more routine class and school endings, while at the other end of the scale, the research on residential care leavers applies to a much smaller group of young people who have probably experienced much more trauma and loss—although I do not want to suggest that this may not be the case for some children in mainstream settings too. So, do these examples have anything in common? The following section makes suggestions and looks at some of the main psychodynamic theoretical contributions to why we find endings difficult.

Theories About Endings

In an ideal world, all children, no matter where they live, will have been gently introduced to the feelings linked to endings, separation, loss and death, but many children do not live in this type of society. Instead, parents and carers have their own 'ghosts in the nursery' (Fraiberg, 1975), as do those who work with children and young people. This means that helping children find their way through these murky waters is dependent on how the adults have navigated these losses in their own lives.

In his classic paper 'Mourning and Melancholia', Freud (1917) laid the groundwork for describing the process of grief and mourning that accompanies bereavement. He explained that although mourning takes time, there could be a healthy or pathological outcome depending on how the individual manages to do the psychological work. In the 'healthy' scenario, people must withdraw the energy from the lost relationship in order to invest it in new people and new activities. The process is not simple nor linear, and the bereaved can move from periods of great despair to injustice or anger, and back again. This rollercoaster of emotions, although painful and disorientating, is a helpful and necessary process.

Julia Samuel (2018), a psychotherapist with an interest in grief, writes about the paradox of getting through the difficult times of life that involve loss and endings, and how even though this is an inevitable aspect of life it is only by experiencing it that people can understand and grow. Until people have processed and reflected on their loss, they cannot really understand their own response in its fullest sense. This is then particularly difficult for children and young people on the edge of school and family life, and in the care system—the very people who are more likely to have experienced early-years loss and trauma and unplanned changes of home setting.

The pathological or complicated scenario means that mourning is hampered usually because the relationship between the deceased and the mourner was hostile or perhaps there were unresolved arguments and other difficulties. It could also be because the mourner feels greatly diminished by the loss and their self-esteem is shattered (Mann-Feder, 2018). Many children on the edge of school and family life may not have experienced actual bereavement, but loss of family and connection through illness, separation, divorce, or imprisonment is likely to play a significant part and stir up these unconscious and painful feelings when other endings arise.

Bowlby's attachment theory, originally developed from work on hospitalised children in the 1950s and the mental health of orphaned children (Bowlby, 1980; Robertson, 1952). The principle is that bonding in infancy and the first year of life is the emotional and social blueprint for all later relationships. Children who develop secure trusting relationships with parents or carers have someone to turn to, someone to help them work things out and a shoulder to lean on. If a child grows up with the experience and belief that other people can help and make things better for them, then they are said to have a secure attachment. This important emotional bedrock helps children and adults manage the sadness of endings. Unfortunately, it is often not the situation for children on the edge of school and family life.

Endings: Planned and Unplanned

Endings that are planned can be talked about and processed, so that the people involved can acknowledge their relationship and the time they have spent together. Sometimes teachers may not acknowledge the significance to pupils of the end of the year and, as mentioned above, anxieties for both staff and pupils are easily stirred up. Even a temporary break needs weeks of preparation, and a final ending of an established good relationship probably needs months. Exactly how long the ending needs to be depends on each person's experience of loss irrespective of whether it is a relationship to a person, a place, a country or a classroom.

However, endings can be complicated if it is too difficult to speak together or the words are too unbearable to hear. A frequent and distressing scenario is also when the ending is sudden or unplanned. The feeling states associated with such endings can be similar to those following a bereavement, such as:

1. **Shock, disbelief, denial.** 'This can't be real.'
2. **Anger** follows loss: 'Why did you leave/abandon me?'
3. **Guilt** at what one should have done differently, at not doing enough, at being too difficult, wasting time, being exhausting.
4. **Despair**, arising from guilt, that it is or may be too late to make reparation.
5. **Grief** at losing the relationship forever.
6. **Sadness** that something of value is coming to an end and pining for what is lost.

Moving through and between these stages is not as streamlined as this list makes it seem, and it certainly takes time.

Many children and young people on the edge of family and school life, especially those in the care system, may have experienced sudden and unplanned endings within their home situation, including birth, foster and adoptive families. That brings with it a whole host of other endings such as school coming to an end abruptly and having to start somewhere else; temporary and permanent exclusions from school; therapy suddenly ending and, of course, separation from friends and peers. These unplanned endings will have an impact on everyone working with them. Here is an example of an unplanned ending from a residential setting.

Practice Example 3

Patrick was taken into care aged three by the police following a particularly torturous episode of domestic violence. The incident lasted a long time, and Patrick witnessed everything as he was locked in the same room with his parents. After that his extreme levels of unpredictable violence meant that numerous foster carers could not help him settle, so when he came to the Mulberry Bush his social worker was unsure what he would manage. Patrick was terrified of everyone, and his fear was such that he could not let himself trust that the staff would be kind to him. His agitation meant that he easily got into fights, punching people in the head. After two years there was an incident where he repeatedly hit a member of staff on the head. A short-term exclusion followed and during that time a joint decision was taken that he should leave. This very rarely happened at the school and was considered an extreme situation. The house manager wrote:

> His placement was brought to a premature end, at which point we were acutely aware that we could easily repeat his early traumatic separation. It is always devastating when a child leaves prematurely. You feel that you have failed, guilty that you have not succeeded in rewriting their experience. I am...once again [...] in touch with the extreme trauma and sense of shame that could seep out of Patrick. The shame, guilt and humiliation that often accompanies children and care. The challenge is how these feelings are acknowledged and worked with at all levels so that they do not become overwhelming and all consuming. It is important to remember that we gave Patrick twenty-two months of security, care and consistency, which was the longest he had experienced in his short life (Oldfield, 2018, p. 140).

Staff were painfully aware that Patrick's violence was a repetition of what he had witnessed as a toddler, and that the decision of the network followed suit by ending his time at the Mulberry Bush prematurely.

Moving Patrick on from school to school was not going to address the underlying issue, but therapeutic work can only succeed when people feel safe, and sometimes saying 'no' is the most helpful things to do. We do not know what it was that led Patrick to re-enact the violence that he had witnessed. Perhaps it was something about the member of staff, or something else that happened at the time. Nevertheless, there would have been a leaving assembly, and offers for reparation between Patrick and the member of staff. Look back to Chap. 5, where we discuss how to understand, process and manage strong feelings.

Pause for thought: Can you think of a child whose ending made you feel as though you had failed or not done enough? Can you think of anything you might have done differently or what you might have done with those painful feelings?

Acknowledged Endings

Endings are commonplace and happen all throughout life. However, any damage or unresolved feelings may be mitigated by talking openly about what is going to happen. This is an example of such a situation.

Practice Example 4

This final practice example looks at a planned and acknowledged ending.

Shona was twelve when Lucy, her foster carer of five years, had to stop looking after her. Lucy was diagnosed with multiple sclerosis, and it was with great reluctance that she had to ask Shona to move out. It was Shona's social worker Steph who facilitated many conversations and skilfully helped Lucy and Shona come to terms with the reality that Lucy's health was having too much of a detrimental impact on family life. Luckily their relationship had improved in the final year. When she went to live with Lucy, Shona would have terrific emotional outbursts that took her a long time to recover from. Lucy's patient and empathic approach meant that gradually Shona would tell Lucy when something was bothering her rather than bottling it all up and exploding with rage. The ending itself turned out to be therapeutic, as Shona was able to see how far she had come since living with Lucy. Lucy was involved in meeting the new foster carers and Shona kept in contact. The whole process took about six months, and during that time Shona was able to say that she was sad and angry with Lucy's illness, but not with Lucy. During those months Shona did regress a bit and had one huge outburst, but she worked out quite quickly what was happening and ended up crying and saying how sad she felt. This is a good example of collaborative working, with everyone involved in Shona's care taking time to reflect on what would be best for her while respecting the solid relational approach of Lucy and Steph.

Leaving Care and Accessing Records

This may seem like an odd topic with which to finish a chapter on endings but leaving the care system can be a challenging time for many young people. Although children go into care for many different reasons, they are likely to have significant feelings about not growing up with their birth family.

Some people who grew up in care have gaps in their childhood memories and have not been able to make sense of what happened, let alone why they were in care in the first place. Accessing care records is one way in which some care leavers may be able to come to terms with the losses involved, and it might be part of the therapeutic process.

The Memory Identity Rights in Records Access project (MIRRA 2017) was set up to research how care records are created and accessed, and one of their recommendations was participatory record-keeping approaches in care settings. The Care Leavers' Association (CLA), a user-led charity to improve the lives of all care leavers, have also worked hard to research and demystify the process of accessing care records.

Practice Example 5

This final practice example is taken from the accounts of two care leavers who describe the difficulties and rewards of accessing their records. The first is from Shirlee, a past Mulberry Bush pupil; the second is from Jim of the Care Leavers' Association.

Shirlee's story: At first I was excited to know that there was information about me, but also worried that it may say I had been a horrible child.

It was with some trepidation that I finally sat with my file in front of me, having declined someone's kind offer to accompany me. I was initially disappointed that there was such little information but also shocked at the language used. It felt so cold and callous. I was repeatedly described as feral, which made me feel dirty if that makes sense. I was heartbroken to learn that I was caught rooting through rubbish bins looking for food when I was only five years old. I was delighted to discover a few letters from my step mum but angry to see there was no input from my dad. There was one birthday card in five years from my birth mother signed 'Barbara (mum)'. This bought up such feelings of animosity towards her, feelings I hadn't felt in over thirty years.

Overall, all it was a huge roller coaster of a day. It left me feeling kind of emotionally overwhelmed and I needed a few weeks to properly digest the little bits of info, and set them straight in my head, and heart. I came away from it feeling sad for the little girl that I had been, grateful for the pitiful scraps of kindness that my step mum showed me in a few letters, and bizarrely, a bit righteous that I was validated in cutting off contact with my dad. It helped me resolve conflicting feelings about him and I feel better for not having such a negative influence in my and my children's lives.

Jim's story: In my case, I was eventually satisfied, but I needed to be persistent in accessing my file and I can understand why some people give up. There is clearly a need for some bureaucracy in all this, but it is off-putting and takes time. The rewards in my case were priceless, but it helps to have support, encouragement and persistence. Many adults who were in care as children have to go through this process alone if they don't know anyone who understands why it matters so much. Even many social workers would struggle to understand why, if my house burnt down tomorrow, the three things I'd grab on the way out would be my photograph collection, my letters and my social services file. So much of my life is bound up in those photocopied papers.

It cannot be emphasised strongly enough what a powerful experience it can be for care leavers to read their files. The effect on individuals reading their case notes is generally underestimated, as is the time it takes to read, digest, re-read and ask further questions of family and friends if possible. It could take someone the rest of their life to fully comprehend what they have read. Also, there is an impact on the facilitator who liaises with care leavers, redacts third party information, and makes sure that the process is undertaken as sensitively as possible, and with regard to policies and procedures. Nowadays there is a trauma-informed approach to this work (Sexton, 2025).

As you reflect on these care leaver accounts, ask yourself what it would be like to read an observer's view of some of the difficult times in your life. First, might it depend on how you had been represented, and whether you felt the observer had adequately portrayed your point of view? A second thought is that putting things on paper could have the effect of solidifying and concretising events and feelings, whereas often people's experience is that the feelings about past events life tend to change over time. Would having a written account change the emphasis of someone's current perspective? All in all, it is likely that seeing someone else's comments about you could be uncomfortable, to say the least.

Conclusion

This chapter has focused on the impact of endings and leaving on children, young people and staff. The practice examples have highlighted how early experiences of a leaving can form someone's ability to manage future endings and why this is a crucial area for children and young people on the edge of school and family life. Everyone has to work out their own way of managing endings, so this is just as important for staff as well.

Perhaps a good place to start is to honestly reflect on your own way of managing endings. If you are someone who finds it difficult, is there something you could do about it? Some people might consider counselling or visiting a bereavement service, whereas others might talk to friends and colleagues who seem to manage it better. How are endings acknowledged and dealt with in your place of work? If there is room for improvement, could you find a way of starting a conversation with your manager and colleagues? Developing one's own self-understanding and then, linked to that, the ability to talk to children and young people about painful subjects, is a tremendous skill to acquire for both personal and professional development.

References

Bowlby, J. (1980). *Attachment and loss. Vol. 3. Loss, sadness and depression*. Hogarth Press and Institute of Psychoanalysis.

Department for Education. (2024). Retrieved August 24, 2025, from https://explore-education-statistics.service.gov.uk/find-statistics/children-looked-after-in-england-including-adoptions/2024

Dixon, J., Cresswell, C., & Ward, J. (2020). *The break staying close, staying connected project evaluation.* Department of Education. Retrieved August 24, 2025, from https://assets.publishing.service.gov.uk/government/uploads/system/uploads/attachment_data/file/931937/Staying_Close_Break.pdf

Fraiberg, S., Adelson, E., & Shapiro, V. (1975). Ghosts in the nursery: A psychoanalytic approach to the problems of impaired infant–mother relationships. *Journal of American Academy of Child Psychiatry, 14*(3), 387–421.

Freud, S. (1917). *Mourning and melancholia.* S. E. 14. Hogarth Press.

Mann-Feder, M. (2018). Where can I mourn? Psychodynamic contributions to working with residential child care. *Journal of Social Work Practice, 32*(4), 463–476.

MIRRA Project. (2017). Retrieved May 15, 2025, from https://blogs.ucl.ac.uk/mirra/2017-2019/

Office for Statistics Regulation (OSR). (2024). Retrieved February 6, 2025, from https://explore-education-statistics.service.gov.uk/find-statistics/suspensions-and-permanent-exclusions-in-england/2023-24-autumn-term

Oldfield, J. (2018). Patrick. Whose shame is it anyway? In J. Diamond (Ed.), *70 years of the mulberry bush school: Showing the way in therapeutic child care* (pp. 131–140). The mulberry bush organisation.

Robertson, J. (1952). *A two-year-old goes to hospital (Film).* Retrieved February 6, 2025, from https://youtube.com/watch?v=s14Q-_BxcU&t=1s

Salzberger-Wittenberg, I. (2013). *Experiencing endings and beginnings* (1st ed.). Routledge.

Samuel, J. (2018). *Grief works: Stories of life, death, and surviving.* Simon and Schuster.

Sexton, A. (2025). Introducing the legacies and trajectories of trauma to the archival field. *Archival Science, 25*(1), 3.

The Care Leavers' Association. Retrieved February 2, 2025., from https://www.careleavers.com/what-we-do/access-to-records/our-stories/jim/

CHAPTER 10

Becoming Research Minded

Caryn Onions, and Heather Price

Introduction

What did you think when you read the title of this chapter? Did you sigh and think, 'that sounds dull'? Or were you curious about how you might become more research minded? Nowadays, most people need to engage with research at work in some way or another. It might be finding out what recent research says about your area of work, or it might be taking part in a research study. Whichever way you encounter research, it is likely to make you think and reflect on your own practice, which is where the journey starts in becoming a research-minded practitioner or organisation.

This chapter explores what we mean by becoming research minded. Irrespective of your setting or professional identity, being research minded probably includes some of the following aspects, which we have divided into four levels. Even though the diagram implies a hierarchy with level 4 representing how research is viewed in the academic and policy arenas, we want to emphasise that in practice there are many important criteria involved in being research-aware such as usefulness in a particular setting, uniqueness to particular projects, inclusiveness of the research process, timeliness and the need to keep costs down (Fig. 10.1).

C. Onions et al., *Supporting Children and Young People with Complex Needs*, Palgrave Texts in Counselling and Psychotherapy, https://doi.org/10.1007/978-3-032-16699-9_10

Fig. 10.1 Levels of research mindedness

Level 1

Usually, practitioners are motivated to discover the best ways of working to achieve the outcomes that they want. You, yourself, have probably carried out online searches, completed reading or been to courses or conferences. Often this searching and curiosity stimulates different solutions or new ways to think about practice. In many organisations, this is a mandatory requirement and for many professionals it is part of their continuous professional development (CPD). We are including foster carers and adopters as, although this is not mandatory, their home-based daily involvement with children is likely to lead to carrying out many informal online enquiries and trying to work out if the advice is evidence-based, as well as having conversations with organisations and other parents in similar situations, and learning in more formal group settings (see Chap. 7).

Level 2

This more focused type of research-minded activity could be action research, which we discuss later in the chapter. This is an established method of enquiry that originated in education (Sagor, 2000) and usually involves a team or group of staff who work together, deciding to investigate new ways of tackling difficulties.

Level 3

The next level of being research minded is where a team, school, residential setting or organisation decides to implement an evidence-based method that includes training all the staff. For example, it could be implementing organisation-wide reflective practice (see Chap. 7), a trauma-informed approach in a children's home, or a teaching-based package such as a phonics programme or maths scheme of work. These initiatives are usually led by the leadership team and have cost and staff training implications. They are likely to be reviewed to make sure they are having an impact.

Level 4

This is where an organisation collaborates with an external researcher or team to explore a specific practice-based question. As with level 3, it implies that the management of the organisation has made the decision to bring in someone external, and that involves budget and time implications. It can also increase reliability and trustworthiness in the research. It is likely to mean that work and practice is observed and/or measured, and it may mean that staff are responsible for collecting data. Depending on the length of the project it might be that staff have to get used to having a researcher around and watching their work or spending additional time providing data. This level of research can feel like an impingement on staff, so it needs careful management.

These levels are simply one way of thinking about different kinds of research. In practice the messiness of life, work, ideas and projects rarely fit into neat categories like these.

> *Pause for thought:* Have you ever been involved in research or evaluation in your organisation in any way? Or have you been a researcher or participant in a study in any other capacity? If you were a participant, did you receive feedback about what had been learnt from the data you contributed?

You may have been a practitioner member of a team evaluating a small or large 'action research' project, or you might have completed an undergraduate or master's dissertation of your own. Perhaps you have filled in questionnaires in relation to sports or health or mental health initiatives in your organisation or local authority, or in relation to a training or parenting programme you attended. Maybe you have been asked to complete questionnaires regarding the mental health and emotional wellbeing of a child in your care such as the Strengths and Difficulties Questionnaire (SDQ) (Goodman, 1997), which local authorities are required to use to assess children looked after aged between four and sixteen.

Researchers are always grateful to participants, as without them their work could not happen. Being a participant can put people on the spot, but there is rarely ever a right or wrong answer and research is always richer with a broad range of perspectives. However, it can also be frustrating for participants when they receive no feedback or have no idea what the outcome was of their involvement, let alone whether they have contributed to practice change. This chapter uses three case studies to explore what it was like for different individuals and organisations to become research minded.

The first case study is of the Coventry Diocese Board of Education (DBE),[1] who worked with the Mulberry Bush and a team of researchers from the University of Sussex, to explore better ways of supporting the social and emotional development, mental health, and wellbeing of the children in some of its schools. The case study ends with an update from the project lead two years later, to see if some of the changes introduced by the research have been sustained.

The second case study is a piece of action research completed by a student undertaking a foundation degree in therapeutic childcare. She was a school nurse looking for a better way of supporting a child in her care who was resistant to medical treatment. The example highlights how the student identified the issue to be researched, engaged with the dilemmas of collecting and reviewing the data, and then made changes to practice.

The final case study looks at how the Mulberry Bush developed a 'social and emotional adjustment scale' ('SEA' Scale). This is a twenty-five-item

[1] Coventry Diocese Board of Education (DBE) has given consent to be named in line with the ethical approval for the research. It is a charity constituted under the Diocesan Board of Education with the responsibility to oversee the Anglican Foundation of 76 Church of England Schools within the diocese of Coventry.

questionnaire devised by a multi-disciplinary group of Mulberry Bush practitioners in collaboration with the University of Sussex. It was developed after staff identified a need for a more nuanced instrument for measuring the emotional and social development of traumatised children like those placed at the Mulberry Bush.

Aims of the Chapter

Through using these three case studies, the chapter

- explores what it means for a workplace to become research minded;
- supports your critical reflection on your stance towards research and its place in your work setting;
- engages with the dilemmas of collecting, using and valuing data; and
- shows how evaluation and research can be supportive for children, families and practitioners.

Case Study 1: The Beacon Project

This first case study outlines how a diocesan family of schools went about becoming research minded. It corresponds to level 4 of the diagram above.

> The Director of Education of the Coventry Church of England Diocese visited seventy-four their diocesan primary schools in the year leading up to the Covid pandemic. These were training event discussions to see how staff and pupils were progressing. The director became more concerned as she repeatedly heard headteachers describe how the psychosocial needs of the children's families were increasing and how the children's struggles were influenced by domestic and community issues as much as educational barriers. The headteachers consistently spoke of pupils who could not cope even with significantly adapted provision, and the school's desire to do more to ensure children could stay within their local community. Understandably, they wanted to avoid school exclusions, realising that it was not a desirable solution for anyone. Alongside this, the director also recognised the existing commitment, skills and hard work of the school communities in responding to the educational, emotional, social and physical needs of pupils and their families. This was a powerful communication and was the motivation for what became the Beacon Project. (Banerjee & Roberts, 2023)
>
> The Beacon Project took place across five primary schools overseen by the Coventry Diocese Board of Education (DBE) during the two years

following the start of the COVID-19 pandemic. This meant that the evaluation had to adjust to the changing circumstances and needs of all of those involved.

How Did the Beacon Project Get Going?

As you can imagine, there are many questions to answer when setting up a research project, even if it is a small one. Some key questions are: What do we really want to find out? What are the costs? Where will the funding come from? What are the ethical considerations of the project? Who are the right people to do the research? It is fair to say that the beginning of any research project consists of many conversations with different people. Networking and speaking with others who have done a similar project helps you not to repeat mistakes and can lead to helpful new contacts. This is an important phase that takes time irrespective of the size of the research project.

The Beacon Project was fortunate in that the Director of Education appointed a project lead who had previously been involved in the team that developed the Social and Emotional Aspects of Learning (SEAL) programme, an initiative that promoted positive behaviour, effective learning and well-being in primary school children (Hallam, 2009). This meant that she already had a contact with an academic at a university in the UK. Also, through a previous job, she had heard about the Mulberry Bush and its interest in children's emotional and social development. Sometimes these contacts are coincidental, but in this case the director of the DBE and the project lead shared an existing and long-term interest in emotional well-being and the research evidence around it.

The next step was to set up contracts of work: a contractual partnership with the Mulberry Bush to provide staff development and support elements of the project, and a contract with the chosen university to undertake the external evaluation. After discussions between the three key players, a project aim was agreed:

> To establish and embed a sustainable approach to the social and emotional development, mental health, and wellbeing of children and young people, both in terms of specialist provision for individuals needing particular support and in terms of universal provision to support the entire school community. (Banerjee & Roberts, 2023)

The project lead now had the task of engaging all the staff in their commitment to the project. Getting staff to become willingly involved in projects like this can sometimes take a lot of work. Participation needs to be encouraged throughout the life of such a project. Parents, carers and children also need to be included.

What Did the Study Consist of?

This ambitious project included a variety of inputs over twenty-four months. First, each of the five schools employed a Family Support Worker (FSW) to offer a family-centred approach to those with complex needs. Second, the Mulberry Bush provided the following resources to all staff, including the FSWs:

- Training in 'behaviour as communication', attachment, neuroscience, trauma and emotion coaching
- Reflective seminars
- FSW group supervision
- Project leads' group supervision
- Six visits to each school per year

The assumption was that these training and CPD activities would generate sustainable changes leading to more emotionally healthy schools that were responsive to emerging issues and more resilient to individual and organisational changes. The participating schools were also invited to take part in the Mulberry Bush pilot of the social and emotional adjustment scale (see below), resourcing the FSWs with planning and evaluating their interventions.

How Did the Researchers Evaluate the Project?

Banerjee and Roberts decided to carry out a 'mixed methods' evaluation, which means they used both quantitative and qualitative research methods in ways that complemented each other.

The quantitative measures were questionnaires completed by children, parents and carers and staff at three different time points at the beginning, middle and end of the two-year project. A project can use questionnaires that already exist in the quantitative research field, or they can devise their own 'bespoke' items in a custom-made design. In each case, the 'instrument' (the questionnaire) needs to accurately measure any change that the project wants to review. The Beacon Project used pre-existing questionnaires that had already been validated. As can happen in 'real world' research, participation in the project tailed off in three of the schools over time, with data from pupils, parents and carers only being fully collected from two of the five schools by the end. However, data from staff was collected throughout.

Statistical analysis of the questionnaires showed that staff reported improved well-being from the start to the middle of the project, and pupils with well-being scores in the lowest third at the start of the project increased significantly from the start to the end. Perhaps disappointingly for the researchers and the project, there were no other significant scores in any of the other tests. This is not unusual in research, and that is why it is helpful to have complementary qualitative data alongside the numerical data.

The qualitative data collection took the form of semi-structured interviews and focus groups. Banerjee and Roberts, both trained in developing and using qualitative methods, wanted to find out how stakeholders viewed the change in support offered by the project for pupils and families, for the staff and others supporting them, and for the general school community. They carried out interviews with the FSWs and they held eleven focus groups with children, parents and carers, and staff in four of the schools. They also had access to the annual leadership reviews conducted by the project lead and a Mulberry Bush former head teacher. The analysis of the interview and focus group data led to some key findings.

The overriding sense from the interviews was that the training had led to a 'deep sense of care and community' (Beacon Project Lead) across all the schools, which translated into improved pupil and staff well-being. Parents, carers and children spoke about feeling less judged in opening up about their difficulties, and staff spoke about being more accepting of these: 'Instead of taking it [bad behaviour] personally as much, you think, "what can I do for this child?" because you see the baggage they are coming with' (Staff member). Parents and carers also felt they were 'working together' with the school, and that staff were also genuinely interested in parental welfare and how things were at home. More trusting relationships were established between home and school. These were the platform on which better solutions to difficulties could be found, building resilience. One parent commented, 'Here, you are speaking to a real person. You know that person is getting to know you, they're going to remember, they're going to tell other people who need to know and then action it.' A child reported, 'The feelings I talk to [the FSW] about are things I don't like. She helps me feel safe.'

How Are Things Two Years Later?

It is only once the data collection is over, the findings have been shared, and the research team has left that one can see if longer-term benefits of a research project are sustained.

In terms of family liaison, the family support worker posts have been continued, despite budget strains. Schools value many aspects of their role, particularly with parents and carers who have previously been hard to reach but are now responsive. Also, FSWs have enabled mainstream placements to continue for pupils with high levels of complex special educational needs. Their presence has also led to reduced stress in staff.

In relation to the reflective culture of the schools, all describe more frequent staff discussions that focus on high-profile pupils and their families. One school has incorporated a regular system for formal staff reflection including termly individual sessions and a weekly collective reflection, while a second school has included formal half-termly reflection for senior leaders. Finally, in two schools, senior leaders describe how dedicated staff reflection sessions have supported decision-making and resilience.

Although routine reflective practice groups have not been established within all the schools, the feedback suggests that staff are communicating more about the challenges of the work. The training they received has improved their understanding and knowledge, while the reflective sessions provided have helped them to trust each other more and to bring a sense of togetherness and belonging to the school communities. Each project school has maintained their drive for the Beacon Project's original aim to support vulnerable children, their families and the wider community so they may live their lives in all their fullness. Finally, the director of Coventry's Diocesan Board of Education is hoping to offer all head teachers facilitated reflective sessions, in order to support leadership resilience across the system of schools and to model wellbeing approaches across the wider organisation.

Case Study 2: Action Research

This case study is of a school nurse, Loretta, who was also a student completing her dissertation. It provides an example of action research as a way of becoming research minded. Action research corresponds to level 2 of the diagram at the start of this chapter and was described by Kurt Lewin (1948) as 'Research which proceeds in a spiral of steps, each of which being composed of planning, action and the evaluation of the result of the action' (Kemmis & McTaggert, 1990, p. 8). This was further developed by Kemmis (2009), who added a fourth element, the art of reflection.

Here is a brief overview of Loretta's starting point, a practice-related issue:

Seven-year-old Kamal's early years of neglect, physical and sexual abuse led to the deterioration of his health. A vital part of his treatment was to receive a fortnightly injection, but Kamal refused to let his foster carer inject him. By the time he was referred to a residential school he had refused treatment for over six months. Loretta was concerned about his health and future prognosis. Also, because of his early years' experiences in his birth family, his self-esteem was very low, and Loretta wondered whether his refusal to have the injections might have been a form of deliberate self-harm.

In order that treatment could be re-started, Loretta suggested to the treatment team and senior leaders in the school that Kamal sat on a care worker's lap and was held still while she did the injection. His social worker had given their consent. However, the staff's response was different. They considered that Loretta's request would have been against the school's guidelines, which are that restrictive physical intervention (RPI) is only allowed where there is the likelihood of self-harm, harming others or significant damage to property. Staff believed that Kamal's right to refuse medication must be respected in line with legislation, including the Human Rights Act (1998) and the European Convention on the Rights of the Child (1989).

Loretta was puzzled and intrigued. Although she was not trained to carry out RPIs in the school, she knew that these interventions were only used as a last resort to safeguard children. However, this differed from her experience of working in a hospital. On a ward if a young child was unable to remain still for clinical procedures they could be physically held by carers providing it was medically necessary and, in the child's best interest. (Brenner, 2007).

In both settings the rationale for using RPIs was the child's safety. Loretta's dilemma was that school practice said, 'don't hold', but the nurse in her was saying 'we need to hold'. As a registered nurse, she had to adhere to the Nursing Midwifery Council (NMC) code (2018) and administer necessary treatment without undue delay (NMC code 1.4). Loretta felt her professional registration was at risk from an act of omission and failure to administer the necessary treatment.

It also became clear that Kamal's birth mother had been responsible for harsh and severe punishments, and when Loretta first tried to support Kamal with his treatment he would say, 'You always want to hurt me, you're just like her' and 'You're meant to care for me, but you don't'. Loretta tried many different approaches such as local analgesia, distraction, play therapy and having his favourite people with him, but to no avail. She did not want to increase Kamal's trauma and further jeopardise their relationship.

How the Action Research Was Undertaken

As part of the action research, Loretta decided to gather the views of the whole staff group to establish if it could ever be appropriate to physically hold a traumatised child during an invasive yet necessary medical procedure. She sent a questionnaire to the whole staff group (100 people) and received twenty-nine replies. Twenty-four of the twenty-nine respondents thought it could be appropriate to 'hold' a child for an invasive clinical procedure, but the number reduced to twenty-one people who would be willing to do that. In addition, Loretta collected Kamal's data from the logging and recording system used by the school to provide a fuller picture of the type and nature of Kamal's physical interventions. She did this to see whether the reluctance to 'hold' Kamal on medical grounds was representative of a global reluctance or something different. She also collected the clinical data related to Kamal's medical condition from the hospital team.

With all the data to hand and because Kamal's chronic illness required long-term invasive treatment, Loretta decided it was an impossible and unrealistic task to eliminate any distress and re-traumatisation altogether. Therefore, she referred Kamal's care to the local hospital, so that treatment could be administered intravenously. This process required hospitalisation, venepuncture, cannulation, blood tests, and being immobile while attached to the infusion. With this treatment regime in place, Kamal's medical condition improved but his anxiety about the treatment increased, and his carers had to find more elaborate ways to help him accept treatment.

Pause for thought: Can you identify things in your work which could be considered action research? If so, are you surprised to see something based on ordinary practice described as research?

Overview of Action Research

There are various models of action research, with broadly the same elements, which are to identify an issue, plan and undertake the action, observe the outcome, reflect and make changes. Initially, Loretta identified Kamal's deteriorating medical condition and his long-term prognosis. She also teased out the various professional, legal and ethical dilemmas of ensuring his treatment took place. She then gathered his medical data and staff attitudes and took the decision to refer him to hospital for treatment. The ending phase consisted of amending the school's Health and Medical Policy to highlight the school's position of not physically intervening if a child refuses medical treatment and all the other ways of encouraging and helping a child to accept treatment.

The tasks that Loretta carried out were within her usual role, and that is one of the useful aspects of action research. It is used to look at practice-based problems and find solutions by trying out sometimes new ways of doing routine tasks. Doing this will be familiar to many of you. It is part of many practitioners' daily work, but most do not see their jobs through this lens and so the existing research mindedness of practitioners is often overlooked.

Case Study 3: Developing the SEA Scale

This final case study focuses on a different type of research and summarises how the Mulberry Bush developed the social and emotional adjustment scale (SEA Scale), a twenty-five-item questionnaire created by a multidisciplinary group of Mulberry Bush practitioners and academics at the University of Sussex (https//sea.scale.org).

Why Was the SEA Scale Created?

In May 2008, the Department for Children, Schools and Families published a framework called Assessing Pupil Progress (APP). Its aim was to support teachers' classroom assessment of National Curriculum levels. It sought to provide a system for teachers to make judgements about the standard of pupils' work and plan future learning activities. Around the same time, a group of senior staff at the Mulberry Bush repeatedly asked themselves the question: 'how do we know whether pupils are making emotional and social progress alongside their academic learning?'. Although there were already some tools/measures in use, they did not embrace the psychodynamic and attachment theory elements of Mulberry Bush practice, plus they tended to be behaviour and symptom based, which is also not in keeping with the Mulberry Bush approach. It was this lack of measures sympathetic to the Mulberry Bush way of working that was the impetus for the SEA Scale.

> *Pause for thought:* What sort of data do you collect in your role? How does this feed back into your practice?

There have been three phases in the development of the SEA Scale to date, which are briefly outlined below to give an idea of how plans and thinking progressed as well as a sense of the time it took to develop and validate a questionnaire. Phase 1 was creating the SEA Scale; phase 2 involved launching the SEA Scale to a group of early users, and phase 3 was gathering more data and validating the questionnaire.

Phase 1: How Did we Develop the SEA Scale?

Based on the APP described above, phase 1 was to devise an Emotional and Social APP. We called it the ESAPP, and it is still in use at the Mulberry Bush school. Initially, we brought together a cross-school group of staff, who, through conversations and team discussions, devised eleven 'key elements' that they considered the most important areas of social and emotional development for the traumatised children in their care. We also identified three 'spine elements': those aspects that underpinned the Mulberry Bush core relationship-based work.

Key Elements

1. Being able to play (spine element)
2. Building healthy and mutually trusting relationships (spine element)
3. Keeping themselves and others safe
4. Asking for help and making use of it
5. Reflecting on and communicating feelings rather than acting them out (spine element)
6. Functioning appropriately in a group
7. Involving themselves appropriately in their care and the care of the environment
8. Improving self-awareness and valuing achievement
9. Making a contribution and becoming involved in the immediate and wider community
10. Being a successful learner
11. Using and applying learnt skill and knowledge

The last part of the first phase involved working on each element so we could find a way of measuring each child's progress on it, as well as planning future activities to support progress on that measure over time. This generated a 198-box grid, something much larger and more impractical than we had envisaged. Soon afterwards, during the coffee break at a conference, we talked about what we were working on and were fortunate to be directed towards a university team of academics who were also interested in social and emotional adjustment. This led to the start of a long and fruitful collaboration where we started to understand the steps that were necessary to transform the unwieldly ESAPP into a more practical assessment tool that could be a properly validated questionnaire. This became the SEA Scale. We began to comprehend the time this would take. The importance and support of a multi-disciplinary team of practitioners and academics working and thinking together on an ambitious project like this cannot be underestimated.

Coming up with the Questions for the SEA Scale

We realised that for the grid to be useful to other related professionals working with traumatised children on the edge of school and family life, it needed to be much shorter. But how were we going to achieve that? An MSc student took on the task of reducing the ESAPP to the briefer twenty-five-item SEA Scale as we know it today (Williamson 2014). Eighteen teachers from the Mulberry Bush school and two mainstream primary schools provided scores for ninety-eight children on the SEA Sale and the Strengths and Difficulties Questionnaire (SDQ; Goodman, 1997).

Factor analysis of the SEA Scale identified three distinct subscales: (i) social and emotional functioning, (ii) externalising/emotion dysregulation, and (iii) response to significant adults. We have since removed the third subscale, but in the future, when we have collected more data, we can reconsider its strength as a factor.

Phase 2: Launching the SEA Scale to Early Users

If the SEA Scale was going to be used and valued by people outside of the Mulberry Bush, we needed to shift our focus to being outward looking. We needed the SEA Scale to become an outward 'product' and therefore we needed feedback on all aspects of it; for example, its useability, visual presentation, scoring system, and so on. There were many meetings and discussions that led to us building a website and developing a version that could be tested outside of the Mulberry Bush. This took a considerable length of time as we started during COVID-19 and had to raise funds for the work needed to shift focus to external users. We have since gathered much invaluable feedback from a group of early users. The overriding outcome was realising that we needed a new website with different functions and capabilities. At the time of writing, we are exploring new avenues for funding from various UK research initiatives and academics to further the project. We are liaising with experts in questionnaire design, as well as those with business-focused expertise. The multi-disciplinary aspect of the SEA Scale project has been core to its development, and significant time has been invested to get to this phase.

Phase 3: Validating the SEA Scale

We developed the SEA Scale because the existing tools did not measure social and emotional adjustment in ways aligned to the Mulberry Bush approach. So that we can feel confident about any future claims, it is important for a questionnaire like the SEA Scale to be valid and reliable. That means it must repeatedly measure what it is supposed to measure. Therefore, it needs to have been trialled a great many times and the findings supported by statistical analysis.

One of the ways of doing this is to obtain more completed questionnaires, and this is what we did in phase 3. The Mulberry Bush has funded a PhD student to further the research and to focus on the use of the SEA Scale in mainstream primary schools to track the social and emotional development of traumatised children. This work is ongoing and we hope to report on the findings in the near future.

Learning Points

The SEA Scale development has been a very long process. Once the PhD findings have been incorporated into the new website, then the project is likely to have taken nearly twenty years. It has been hugely rewarding, but also time consuming and expensive. Finding the right people to support the process has been invaluable, plus it has been a great example of collaborative work (see Chap. 7). The overall process has included aspects of each of the four levels of research, which is what has made it a rich research experience for the organisation.

Conclusion

We hope this chapter has piqued your interest in research and its relevance for practice. The chapter started with an overview of some of the ways in which practitioners, parents and carers can become research minded. We consider research-mindedness to be anything from attending an online webinar through to commissioning or partnering with a team of external researchers, and everything in between. Working with academic colleagues or under their direction can be hugely professionally rewarding, but it often needs management support. Most of the examples mentioned in this chapter will have a cost and time implication, and these need to be factored in at the start. However, building one's own research mindedness can also be taken forward at an individual or small group level, starting with attending a CPD activity and deciding to ask more searching questions about its content, or undertaking a small-scale 'action research' study project or evaluation to solve a problem one has encountered in practice.

> *Pause for thought:* How might you become more research minded? What might you need to develop and embed a research culture in your organisation? Where might you get support for this?

References

Banerjee, R, & Roberts, L. (2023). *The beacon project evaluation: Final report.* Retrieved July 12, 2025, from https://coventrydbe.org/resources/

Brenner, M. (2007). Child restraint in the acute setting of paediatric nursing, an extraordinarily stressful event. *Issues in Comprehensive Paediatric Nursing., 30*(1–2), 29–37.

European Convention on the Rights of the Child. (1989). Retrieved July 12, 2025, from https://www.unicef.org.uk/what-we-do/un-convention-child-rights/

Goodman, R. (1997). The Strengths and Difficulties Questionnaire: A research note. *Journal of Child Psychology and Psychiatry, 38*, 581–586.

Hallam, S. (2009). An evaluation of the Social and Emotional Aspects of Learning (SEAL) programme: Promoting positive behaviour, effective learning and well-being in primary school children. *Oxford Review of Education, 35*(3), 313–330.

Human Rights Act. (1998). Retrieved July 12, 2025, from https://www.legislation.gov.uk/ukpga/1998/42/contents

Kemmis, S. (2009). Action research as a practice-based practice. *Educational Action Research., 17*(3), 463–474.

Kemmis, S., & McTaggert, R. (1990). *The Action Research Planner.* Deakin University Press.

Lewin, K. (1948). *Resolving Social Conflicts; Selected Papers on Group Dynamics.* (G. W. Lewin, Ed.). Harper & Row.

Sagor, R. (2000). *Guiding school improvement with action research.* Association for Supervision and Curriculum Development.

The Nursing and Midwifery Council Code. (2018). Retrieved July 12, 2025, from https://www.nmc.org.uk/globalassets/sitedocuments/nmc-publications/nmc-code.pdf

Williamson, J. (2014). *Investigating and examining the Mulberry Bush Social and Emotional Adjustment Scale.* Unpublished dissertation. University of Sussex.

CHAPTER 11

Concluding Thoughts

Caryn Onions, Heather Price, and Dave Roberts

As we were preparing the final manuscript for this book (Autumn 2025), media reports were arriving daily, warning about rising levels of need, falling budgets, and a reduction in levels of support services for our children and young people. As individuals or organisations, we cannot usually reduce the level of need or reverse all the budget cuts, but we can review our practice to improve the impact of our work with children, families, teams and networks. The authors of this book believe that, in the UK, we desperately need our education and care systems to shift their focus towards a genuine relationship-based, inclusive approach.

In the Introduction, we argued that building individual trusting relationships is core to taking a therapeutic approach with children and young people who struggle with school and family life. This might not seem such a ground-breaking insight and is often commonly acknowledged. But in the rest of the book, we have sought to unpack why the apparently simple task of relationship-building can be so demanding, and to provide a detailed answer regarding what is needed to sustain it. Above all, building trusting relationships takes time, alongside parallel support for the key individuals tasked with holding the child or young person in mind.

C. Onions et al., *Supporting Children and Young People with Complex Needs*, Palgrave Texts in Counselling and Psychotherapy,
https://doi.org/10.1007/978-3-032-16699-9_11

An overarching theme in the book is the emotionally mindful availability of the practitioner. This is multifaceted and includes the personal effort and wider support needed to sustain their ongoing awareness of the therapeutic needs of the child or young person. The sensitively 'in touch' professional will be more attuned to the emotional needs of those in their care, together with their own needs, which means they will be better able to offer support, and help children recognise their own feelings and emotions.

In Chap. 2, we explained the Mulberry Bush's 'triangle' of three core principles supporting the emotionally available practitioner: a psychodynamic approach, reflective practice, and collaborative working. Here, we offer our concluding thoughts about each of these principles. In each chapter they have acted as core anchor points, informing the work with children and young people.

Chapter 2 introduced 'Tom', a 1960s Mulberry Bush pupil who shattered windows as his anxiety rose on not hearing from his birth mother. It took time for staff to make sense of this behaviour, because on the surface it looked as if Tom was being simply angry and rebellious. A psychodynamic approach assumes a child's behaviour is linked to their feelings, which may sit under the surface of awareness. The psychodynamic approach runs throughout the chapters in the rest of the book and is addressed in detail in Chap. 4, on 'behaviour as communication'. The author makes the important point that, more often than not, children and young people do not know why they are behaving as they are. An example is given of fourteen-year-old Bailey, who is underachieving at secondary school. Asking for explanations or simply expecting Bailey to put more effort in or putting an intervention in place without building a connection to the young person is unlikely to be effective. Both Chap. 4, Behaviour as Communication, and Chap. 5, What to Do About Strong Feelings?, suggest ways of thinking about children's behaviour that can be applied in any setting. When we see behaviours that might challenge us, instead of wondering 'How do I stop this?', the authors suggest we ask, 'What is happening for that individual?'. Consistently seeing behaviour as a communication of a feeling helps us work out how to respond. We often need to set limits and boundaries to keep people and property safe, but we do this while taking into consideration the meaning for the child of their behaviour.

Chapter 3, New Beginnings, addresses the need for the practitioner to have space for reflective practice that is ongoing and personalised, and takes account of the emotional impact of work with children who are 'turned against the system'. The importance of space for reflection is the second principle anchoring thinking throughout the book. The fruits of having space to reflect can feed into a more attuned approach, as in the example given in Chap. 3 of Dean, who struggles with transitions and is about to go into Year 5. His school have thought ahead to arrange lunchtime chess sessions with the Year 5 teacher, Mr. Tompkins, in the year prior to the transfer.

Chapter 5, What to Do About Strong Feelings?, also underlines the emotional pressures on the practitioner or carer and the counterintuitive idea following from properly acknowledging this, that non-judgemental therapeutic work needs to begin with the adult supporting the child. We are aware that not all organisations encourage depth-level reflection for practitioners, and perhaps this is particularly the case in educational settings. We also acknowledge that for some carers and professionals, this way of working might be completely new, and to others may seem alien, threatening, or otherwise inappropriate. Nevertheless, throughout the book we have emphasised the need for people working and caring for children and young people with complex needs to develop their own ability to self-reflect. This maximises our ability to be open to our blind spots, challenges our assumptions and biases, and hopefully enables us to keep the feelings of children and young people at the centre of what we do.

Chapter 5 explicitly acknowledges that some adults caring for children and young people, such as adoptive parents, struggle to access meaningful support in a family context, where the physical and psychological safety of everybody in the setting is harder to maintain than in an organisation. The example is given of nine-year-old Lianna, who is physically violent towards her adoptive mother. A similar example, of twelve-year-old Logan, who is violent towards his grandmother, is presented in Chap. 6, Working Things Out with Children and Families. Chapter 6 also notes the professional development of professionals or carers, and the author acknowledges that at the start of her own professional career as a social worker she would not have been well-equipped to use a trauma-informed approach to support her clients. The chapter closes with the example of Angie, a school counsellor at Greenfields Secondary School, who, with supervisory support, has been able to identify twelve-year-old Emily's emotionally based school avoidance as being connected to 'stuck' feelings related to the suicide of her father, rather than to bullying.

We have argued in this book that the need for professional therapeutic reflective support for any adult undertaking specialist re-parenting and education should be properly understood and recognised. We have also sought to clarify that reflective spaces or groups, and supervision, are not the same as personal therapy or having a place for 'moaning and dumping'—they need to be child-focused and informed by an appropriate theoretical model. But we believe that encouraging parents, carers and staff to share their experiences and feelings in a safe setting where this is genuinely valued can truly make a difference to practice and to the lives of the children and young people. It makes the helper feel less alone and can enable them to hold on to the hope that things can get better, giving them renewed energy for building the relationship with the child.

Chapter 7, Supporting Staff, addresses further external and internal pressures that mitigate against proper professional support. We need leadership in our different organisations that recognises and prioritises spaces that allow staff and carers to explore the impact of the work, in order to manage the intense feelings that can arise. To return each day, or to live with the complex emotional states of the children and young people we care for, requires parents, carers and educators, and their organisations, to be emotionally attuned. The support does not need to be heavily resource-reliant, but it does require a shift in how people think about leadership for support. Chapter 10, Becoming Research Minded, gives an example of strong leadership and a shift in focus in this area. Head teachers participating in the Beacon Project introduced Family Support Workers (FSWs) into primary schools in Coventry (fortuitously, just before the pandemic) to support the emotional, social, mental health and well-being of the children and families. Reflective practice groups became integral for all staff, not just the new FSWs. This meant that pastoral tasks became everyone's responsibility.

Collaboration, the third and final Mulberry Bush principle introduced in Chap. 2, is mentioned in Chaps. 6, 7, and 9, but outlined in depth in Chap. 8. This chapter notes the constant calls for 'working together' and 'joined up thinking' in safeguarding, education and social care policy across many decades. The repeated exhortation for this to happen indicates how complex collaboration within and across organisations and systems can be. Every different professional and non-professional member of the team around a child will have pieces of the jigsaw puzzle which when brought together, will illuminate a 'whole picture' of the child and their circumstances; new understandings can emerge at the boundary of different parties' views.

Chapter 8 also draws attention to every professional or carer's investment in their own role. Boundary-setting plus flexing or adapting, can take time and a lot of reflection, not least because doing so can feel like a wound to an individual's professional identity. The example given of eleven-year-old Zack, and his special school teaching assistant, Maryanna, illustrates this. Maryanna did not feel empowered to suggest an alternative strategy for supporting Zack, who was receiving a lot of interventions and was often physically restrained on the way to or from class. Maryanna reports on how much 'time, bribery and arm-twisting' it took to gain permission from relevant professional parties above her in the hierarchy to be acknowledged as 'the expert in Zack'. She notes how one part of her solution, tea and biscuits and a bit of maths work with the caretaker, was controversial because it threatened established roles and ways of working, although it was successful.

Working collaboratively enables people who are different from each other to think together and point out habits and blind spots that individuals have stopped noticing long ago. When we collaborate, we must let go of some things we have worked for, otherwise it is not collaboration. Linked to that, we must be open to other people's views and opinions and work on shared problems rather than seeing other people's differing views as the problem.

Pause for thought: Consider the three key anchoring ideas informing this book: a psychodynamic approach, reflective practice, and collaborative working. What new messages have you taken from the book in relation to each of these areas? Pick one area and note how you might use a new insight in your practice.

Finally, we would like to underline an implicit theme running throughout the book: it takes a long time for children and young people on the edge of school and family life to find a way through and start to grow and recover. Our experience is that the families and networks of such children and young people often do not fully appreciate the time it takes to assess children's therapeutic needs, and then the actual timescale for change. Much of the collaborative work is helping staff, parents and carers understand what it may be achievable for children with a high number of adverse childhood experiences and a realistic timeframe. For many children and young people, change can be slow and may not become apparent until adulthood.

Governmental and policy frameworks rarely recognise this aspect of the therapeutic approach and support needed. All too often, if some support has been provided but there is no short-term change, the focus of mental health, educational or social service provision can move from support to discharge, exclusion and a more punitive approach. However, as practitioners working on the ground, our task is to hold the potential of each child and young person in mind, even when their behaviour is not changing over the short term and they themselves do not have self-belief. We firmly believe that despite the great challenges of the work, there are deep personal rewards that come from seeing our children and young people grow. A belief in the possibility of change is what keeps us in the work. Occasionally we are lucky enough to receive confirmation from the people in our care that we have been working along the right lines. We will end with something that an ex-pupil said about their time at the Mulberry Bush:

> *I do struggle with anger issues I'm not going to lie, but that's helped me shape who I am…. and no one wanted to change who I am, they wanted to work with who I am, and there's been so many adults in my life who haven't been able to achieve this but they somehow managed to do it with me and that's what I really want to thank them for.*

Glossary[1]

Academy trust An academy trust is a charity responsible for overseeing and governing a group of schools.

Action research A type of small-scale research that seeks to effect change rather than just describing a situation. Action research normally follows a series of stages such as identifying a theme to investigate; Plan intervention; Act; Observe; Reflect; Repeat process.

Adverse Childhood Experiences (ACE) Adverse childhood experiences are potentially traumatic events that occur during childhood (0–17) and can have lasting effects on physical and psychological health leading to chronic health conditions in adulthood. Examples include abuse (physical, emotional, sexual); neglect; living in a household with domestic violence, substance or alcohol misuse or criminal behaviour; or living with a caregiver with mental illness.

Attachment disorder Attachment disorder affects a person's ability to form and maintain secure emotional bonds. It often arises within the home context.

[1] This glossary contains several definitions based on diagnostic manuals typically used in psychiatry. We view these as medical categories that can be helpful but are not a total description of a child.

C. Onions et al., *Supporting Children and Young People with Complex Needs*, Palgrave Texts in Counselling and Psychotherapy,
https://doi.org/10.1007/978-3-032-16699-9

Attention deficit hyperactivity disorder (ADHD) ADHD is a named disorder / mental health diagnosis characterised by impulsivity, inattention and hyperactivity.

Autism Autism or autism spectrum disorder/continuum is characterised by differences in social interaction and communication, sometimes including restrictive or repetitive patterns of behaviour or interests.

Behaviour as communication This phrase refers to the idea that people unconsciously communicate their feelings, thoughts and attitudes through their behaviour as a means to meet an unmet need. It can be verbal and/or non-verbal.

CAMHS Child and Adolescent Mental Health Services.

Childhood trauma Childhood trauma refers to events that threaten a child's sense of safety, well-being and self-esteem. They can have a profound and long-lasting effect.

Compassion fatigue Compassion fatigue relates to the emotional impact of caring/working with the emotional pain/trauma of others. More specifically, it refers to when an individual struggles emotionally, physically and psychologically from helping others as a response to prolonged stress or trauma.

Conduct disorder Conduct disorder is characterised by persistent challenging and anti-social behaviour across different settings.

Conscious The awareness of your own thoughts, feelings, experiences or actions.

Containing/containment Containment describes a relational process in which one person, usually an adult, can consider/take in/understand a child's experience, digest or process the intolerable/difficult feeling, and hand it back to the child in a way that makes it more tolerable to them, in the way a caregiver may think through, make sense of and soothe a tiny, non-verbal baby. In this way, the adult contains some of the emotional experience of the child.

Countertransference Countertransference describes the unconscious process in which our own feelings and thoughts are triggered by a child's transference and may influence our interactions with, and feelings towards, a child. For example, when a child is repeatedly rejecting, it may activate retaliatory feelings in one person, for their own unconscious reasons, and in another, it may activate hurt and depressed feelings. To make sense of the countertransference, we need to know ourselves very well and to have worked hard to understand the child.

Culture The term culture is used to refer to the customs, ideas, values and social behaviours of an organisation.

Defence mechanisms/Defences These are strategies we use unconsciously that protect us from the anxiety we feel about unacceptable feelings and thoughts. They include denial, displacement, identification, repression, rationalisation, projection, regression and isolation.

Dyslexia Dyslexia is a learning disorder characterised by difficulties processing information that affects, among other areas, reading, writing and spelling.

Emotion coaching Emotion coaching is an evidence-based approach to help children to understand and manage their emotions. It enables adults to co-regulate children's emotions, de-escalate situations where behaviour is challenging, and develop children's ability to self-regulate their own emotions and behaviour.

Emotional regulation Emotional regulation is a person's ability to recognise, manage and respond to their emotions.

Emotionally based school avoidance This is a term used to describe a child or young person who has severe difficulty in attending school due to emotional factors. This can result in prolonged absences from school.

Evidence based Evidence based refers to ways of working that are informed by empirical evidence, often research and data analysis.

Factor analysis Factor analysis is used in research to refer to a statistical method for identifying underlying relationships among a large set of variables.

Fight, flight, freeze and fawn These terms refer to physiological responses to stress or what is perceived to be a harmful situation. Fight—a response that involves aggressively confronting the threat. Flight—a response to avoid/escape the threat. Freeze—the person becomes unable to act or is 'frozen'. Fawn—the response involves trying to appease the source of threat as a way to avoid harm.

Group supervision Group supervision is a group process to help group/team members learn from each other, get peer support and reflect on their work as a team.

Hold/holds See Restraint / RPI

Holding in mind An intentional and emotional holding someone in your mind.

Insecure attachment style Attachment is the result of the innate human predisposition for infants to caregivers. It is part of the biological basis of survival. Disturbance or disruption of the initial attachment bond with a primary caregiver can lead to insecure attachment.

Internal Working Model John Bowlby's theory whereby the child creates a blueprint of themselves in relation to others based on their experiences of being parented.

Intervention An intervention is a planned action/series of actions intended to change a situation.

Life story work Life story work is a planned piece of work to help care experienced children and young people understand their own history and life story.

Mentalization Mentalization is the ability to understand the mental state of oneself and others, and realise how this is affecting the emotions, thoughts and actions of ourselves and others. This understanding of our own perspectives as well as those of other people leads to more successful interactions and social relationships.

Networking Refers to making connections and relationships between individuals or organisations.

Neurodiversity Neurodiversity refers to the range of differences in individual brain function and behavioural traits, regarded as part of normal variation in the human population (used especially in the context of autistic spectrum disorder/continuum).

Nurture group A nurture group is a focused, short-term intervention for primary or secondary school pupils with social, emotional and behavioural difficulties that make it harder for them to learn in a mainstream class.

Projection Projection is an unconscious defence mechanism that is used to protect ourselves from feelings that we experience as intolerable. It involves attributing to others, feelings or traits that belong to us so we can avoid the uncomfortable feelings.

Projective identification A process whereby individuals and groups expel parts of themselves into another person or object and unconsciously identify with the projected material seen in others. The person or object is then experienced as if it were the projected content. It is also understood as a primitive means of communication.

Psychodynamic A psychodynamic approach looks at the ways in which early childhood and other past experiences shape our understanding of the world, our experiences and our relationships. It focuses on how these experiences affect us in unconscious ways, which in turn influence our behaviour and impacts how we experience ourselves and others.

Randomised control study A randomised control study is a type of research where participants are randomly allocated to an experimental group or control group to assess the effectiveness of an intervention.

Reframe Finding a benign motive for behaviour, and giving the same described behaviour a different meaning. E.g. behaviour seen as naughty (existing frame) is seen as communicative (reframe).

Reflection / reflective practice Reflective practice is a term that refers to the professional ability of reviewing one's actions so as to engage in the process of continuous learning.

Relational / relationship-based practice Relational practice is the deliberate, organisation-wide commitment to building strong, respectful relationships between all individuals to create emotionally safe environments.

Restraint (RPI) / physical Intervention Restraint (often referred to as Restricted Physical Intervention) refers to the use of minimum-required force as part of a deliberate planned restriction of another person's movement to reduce danger or physical harm. Physical intervention refers to providing a child with varying degrees of freedom or mobility, such as leading or guiding them.

SDQ (Strengths and Difficulties Questionnaire) The SDQ is a short behavioural screening questionnaire for children that can be used to assess children's mental health.

Self-regulate The ability to manage one's emotions, behaviours and physiological responses to stress.

Social, emotional and mental health difficulties (SEMH) Social, emotional and mental health difficulties often manifest as problems managing emotions and behaviour, and are a type of Special Educational Needs.

Subscales A component part of a larger scale. Subscales can be used to improve the precision and depth of a study.

Supervision Supervision is the process of professional learning and development, enabling people to gain knowledge, skills and competence, through regular support with an experienced colleague.

Therapeutic relationship A therapeutic relationship is the trusting and collaborative bond that develops between a worker/therapist/practitioner and a child or young person. It is at the core of all therapeutic work.

Therapeutic setting / milieu A setting designed to support healing and growth for individuals who have experienced trauma, through the use of relationships.

Tools / measures Refers to a variety of resources and methods that researchers use to collect, analyse and make sense of data.

Transference Transference is a form of projection and describes the way a child might transfer their experiences of early relationships onto people in the present.

Transition Transition refers to the periods of change we all experience. These may be something or someone moving, or something altering in one way, small or big.

Trauma-informed Trauma-informed refers to an approach that recognises the impact of trauma on all aspects of a child or young person's development. It is sensitive to the person's unique needs, context and culture.

Treatment team A multi-disciplinary team at the Mulberry Bush working together to discuss and plan a child's treatment plan. It could include keyworker, teacher, teaching assistant, home manager or therapist.

Unconscious The unconscious is the part of the mind that is not directly available to us. Psychodynamic theory suggests that we have many thoughts and feelings that we are not aware of that influence our current experience of the world around us, of relationships and our behaviour. Many of our early experiences are stored in memory in the unconscious part of the mind.

Unconditional positive regard The basic acceptance and support of an individual, regardless of how they behave or what they say.

Index

C. Onions et al., *Supporting Children and Young People with Complex Needs*, Palgrave Texts in Counselling and Psychotherapy,
https://doi.org/10.1007/978-3-032-16699-9

The manufacturer's authorised representative in the EU is Springer Nature Customer Service Centre GmbH, Europaplatz 3, 69115 Heidelberg, Germany. If you have any concerns regarding our products, please contact ProductSafety@springernature.com

Printed and bound by CPI Group (UK) Ltd, Croydon, CR0 4YY
17/09/2026
02218434-0001